KU-402-576

SIMPLE ASIAN KITCHEN

Watch then cook with Ming Tsai

Ming Tsai and Arthur Boehm

Photography by Bill Bettencourt

KYLE BOOKS

Dedications

Ming Tsai
For my sons David and Henry, the two reasons I keep trying
to make the world a happier place.

Arthur Boehm
For Richard Getke. And for C. and P.

First published in Great Britain in 2013 by Kyle Books
an imprint of Kyle Cathie Limited
23 Howland Street
London W1T 4AY
generalenquiries@kylebooks.com
www.kylebooks.com

10 9 8 7 6 5 4 3 2 1

ISBN 978 0 85783 090 6

Newcastle Libraries & Information Service	
C4 698984 00 BD	
Askews & Holts	Feb-2013
641.595	£18.99

Text © 2012 by Ming Tsai
Photographs © 2012 by Bill Bettencourt
Book design © 2012 by Kyle Cathie Ltd

Ming Tsai is hereby identified as the author of this work in accordance with
Section 77 of the Copyright, Designs and Patents Act 1988.

All rights reserved. No reproduction, copy or transmission of this
publication may be made without written permission. No paragraph
of this publication may be reproduced, copied or transmitted save
with the written permission or in accordance with the provision
of the Copyright Act 1956 (as amended). Any person who does
any unauthorised act in relation to this publication may be liable to
criminal prosecution and civil claims for damages.

Project editor Anja Schmidt
Designer Jacqui Caulton
Photographer Bill Bettencourt
Prop styling Aaron Michael Caramanis
Copy editor Liana Krissoff
Production by Gemma John and Nic Jones

A Cataloguing in Publication record for this title is available from the British Library.

Colour Reproduction by Alta Image
Printed and bound in China by C & C Offset Ltd

Contents

Introduction

As a chef, I love bringing something new to the table. So I'm really happy to present this book. Not only does it deliver great, easy recipes, but for the first time you also get . . . me.

I'd better explain. Each of the recipes has its own accompanying video showing you how to make the dish. Which means you can have your own personal sous-chef, me again. You also get a complete shopping list for the recipe, so no more scribbled-on scraps of paper to bring to the supermarket.

How did the book come about? All my adult life I've been teaching people how to cook, in my cookbooks and on my TV shows. I'm always thrilled when people approach me and tell me they love my dishes. (I'm happiest when people tell me they've tweaked my recipes, which means they're *really* cooking.) The books are about teaching and so are the shows. The shows add 'pictures' to words. Now you get book and show in one. My tips on ingredients and techniques, the way I plate a dish, everything that's best conveyed through seeing, you can now see alongside this book.

But even without the videos, the book alone is a mighty tool. It's organised by food types, like seafood and poultry, and, as ever, it emphasises simplicity and technique. For the first time, though, I've put my love of entertaining on the page in the form of three special chapters. The first, Platters, provides recipes for hors d'oeuvres and other starters that help make a party go. There's even a section that tells you how to conduct your own sushi-making party, for which your guests make and plate their own maki. I've had such parties and, believe me, they break the ice fast.

The other 'entertaining' chapters are on sweets and cocktails. In Sweets, I present great party desserts like Lemongrass Panna Cotta and Cardamom Chocolate Cake. In Cocktails, I introduce some of the great drinks we make and serve at my restaurant Blue Ginger. If you want to start a party with a bang, any of my cocktails will do it. Mixed drinks are all the rage, and those I present, like the Sake Cucumber Martini and Passion Fruit Mai Tai, are rage-worthy indeed.

Many of us are eating less meat, or have given it up entirely. I've never thought of vegetable dishes as a compromise. Worldwide, the range of non-meat dishes is vast and delicious, and it's a great treat (as well as a challenge) to create my own contenders. Vegheads and meat-eaters alike will enjoy dishes like Hunan Glazed Aubergine with Rice and Three-Mushroom and Jicama Chow Mein.

Ultimately, my goal is to get people to cook. This book's innovations should encourage people to do just that. Nothing, I believe, is more rewarding than cooking for family and friends. The better people eat, the happier they are. and the happier they are, the better. I'm betting that this book will aid the cause.

How to use this book

It's easy and we've given you three ways:

1. Download a QR code reader to your mobile device, scan the QR code of the recipe you're interested in and you'll be taken to the In Your Kitchen landing page on ming.com, where you can sign up. Then you can download the recipe's shopping list for free and choose to watch the video. (The first two videos of each chapter are free; after that there is a small charge per video.) You only need to sign up once – thereafter you'll be automatically directed to the recipe you desire.

2. No mobile device? No problem. Just type the URLs that run along the bottom of each recipe into your computer's browser and you'll get to the same place and sign up as above.

3. Most simply, go to ming.com and click on the In Your Kitchen tab and navigate from there.

Storecupboard

OILS AND VINEGARS

Rapeseed (Canola) Oil. My oil of choice for most cooking. Expressed from rapeseed, the oil is lower in fat (it contains about 6 per cent) than any other vegetable oil. It also contains omega-3 fatty acids. I prefer it not only for health reasons but for its clean 'neutral' flavour.

Rice Vinegar. A delicate, lightly acidic vinegar, white to golden in colour. Rice vinegar should be naturally brewed and unflavoured – check labels. I prefer organic brands, like Wan Ja Shan.

Truffle Oil. Made from olive oil or a mixture of olive and other oils, this versatile ingredient is infused with black or white truffles. It imparts a rich, earthy truffle flavour to a variety of savoury dishes. The brand I like is Terre di Tartufo White Truffle Oil.

Toasted Sesame Oil. This amber-coloured, richly flavoured oil, a staple of the Chinese storecupboard, is used for seasoning only. Don't confuse it with refined, almost colourless sesame oils, which can be used for dressings and cooking.

NOODLES, RICE AND WRAPPERS

Banana Leaves. These natural wrappers, used to enclose food for steaming, impart a subtle anise flavour. They come fresh or frozen – fresh are best. Rinse and dry fresh leaves before using them, and cut away fibrous stems. Defrost frozen leaves at room temperature and unfold them carefully. Wipe all banana leaves before using them with a damp cloth. Look for banana leaves among the frozen foods in Asian, Hispanic or speciality food stores or from online suppliers.

Fresh Noodles or Chow Mein Noodles. Fresh wheat-flour and egg noodles that are used to make chow mein and other dishes. Don't confuse these with the crisp noodles often served in Chinese restaurants for munching or to be sprinkled on stir-fries.

Lumpia Wrappers. Used traditionally in Philippine cooking to make spring rolls, these wrappers are made principally from flour, cornflour and eggs. Sometimes sold as egg roll wrappers or spring roll shells, they're most often available in 312g packets.

Mu Shu Wrappers. These round wrappers are made from wheat flour and tapioca starch. Usually sold frozen, defrost them at room temperature before using.

Mung Bean Noodles. Also called cellophane and bean thread noodles, these fine, translucent noodles are made from ground mung beans. The noodles are never cooked, but are soaked in water until pliable. They're sold dry in packets that range from 25–450g.

Nori. These thin dried seaweed sheets are used primarily to make maki, the Japanese rolls that contain rice and other fillings. Buy toasted nori (labelled *yaki nori*), which are sold flat in packets. Iridescent black, dark green or purplish, nori, if not used immediately, should be wrapped in cling film and stored in a cool, dark place.

Rice Stick Noodles. This widely available thin, flat noodle is one of a large family of rice noodles, both fresh and dried.

Rice Vermicelli. Long, thin and round, these noodles take their English name from the Italian pasta called 'little worms'. They're mostly available in 450g bags.

Shanghai Noodles. An egg noodle that's medium thin and usually sold in 450g bags. If you can't find them, substitute any thick dried or fresh spaghetti.

Rice Paper Wrappers. Known also as *banh trang*, these Vietnamese wrappers are made from a rice plant product. They're used for preparing spring rolls, uncooked or fried. They're most commonly available in 350g packets of 8 round wrappers, and must be soaked briefly before using.

Sushi Rice. Ideal for making sushi because of its moderately sticky texture when cooked, short-grained sushi rice is widely available. Calrose and Kokuho are two quality brands of sushi rice, grown in the USA. Labelling is sometimes inexact. 'Japanese rice', 'new rice' or 'variety rice' are 'sushi rice' alternatives. The most highly regarded Japanese sushi rice is *koshihikari*.

Wonton Wrappers. Flour- and egg-based, these come round or square, thick or thin. Wontons require round wrappers. I recommend the thinnest ones you can find, usually labelled 'extra thin'. The wrappers can be refrigerated for up to 1 week, or frozen for about 2 months.

SEASONINGS, CONDIMENTS AND AROMATICS

Agave Syrup. Produced in Mexico and South Africa, this product of the agave plant, which is also used to make tequila, is similar to honey, but lighter and more 'neutral' in taste. There are two kinds of the syrup, sometimes sold as agave 'nectar', light and dark. The former is milder, and the one I recommend for the recipes in this book.

Fermented Black Beans. This pungent ingredient, used throughout China, is made from partially decomposed soya beans that are dried and then salted. Sold most often in plastic bags, they last indefinitely if stored in a cool, lightless place. Rinse the beans before using to remove excess salt.

Five-Spice Powder. A traditional Chinese seasoning blend usually composed of equal parts ground cinnamon, star anise, cloves, fennel and Szechuan peppercorns. With a fragrant, 'warm-cool' flavour, the spice goes particularly well with fatty meats like pork and duck. The spice is thought to be healthy, as the number five is considered meaningful in Chinese belief.

Fish Sauce. Called *nam pla* in Thailand and *noc mam* in Vietnam, this Southeast Asian staple is made from salted and fermented anchovies. Once opened, keep fish sauce in the fridge.

Chinese Hot Mustard Powder. The ground product of pungent mustard seeds, this is mixed with water before using. It's available from some supermarkets and Asian food stores.

Ketjap Manis. A syrupy, dark brown Indonesian seasoning made from soya beans, palm sugar and other ingredients, including garlic. Similar to soy sauce, but sweeter and with a more complex flavour than most soy sauce types, it's available in Asian food stores.

Korean Chilli Pepper Flakes. Known in Korea as *gochugaru*, this incendiary seasoning is made from sun-dried thin chillies. It's available in Asian food stores. Once opened, store the pepper in a jar in the fridge.

Madras Curry Powder. All curry powders are spice blends. My preferred type and brand is labelled 'Madras curry powder', a mixture that's favoured in the southern Indian state from which it derives its name. It has a mellow balance that's neither too hot nor too mild. Look for brands in which bits of bay leaf are visible, and use it only when it's fresh.

Mirin. This essential Japanese ingredient is made from rice wine and sugar. It adds a touch of sweetness to many dishes and is also used as a glaze. I recommend naturally brewed *hon-mirin*. It contains natural sugars rather than sweeteners like corn syrup, which is found in *agi-mirin*, an alternative type.

Miso. The defining ingredient of the eponymous Japanese soup, miso is a savoury seasoning paste made from rice, barley and/or soya beans. For the recipes in this book, I call for *shiro miso*, which is made from rice. It's available in cans, jars, tubs and plastic bags, and is best stored in the fridge, where it lasts up to 3 months.

Natural Garlic Powder. In my experience, natural garlic powder, which is free from additives, is superior to other kinds, which can be acrid or otherwise taste 'off'. I use natural garlic and onion powders for spice rubs, where the fresh kind would not work as well, if at all. All garlic and onion powders must be fresh. If natural garlic powder is not available, look for organic.

Organic Worcestershire Sauce. Most of us are familiar with traditional Worcestershire sauce, a piquant tamarind-based flavouring and condiment. Recipes for the commercial organic type vary widely, but the sauce usually contains the defining tamarind, soy or tamari sauce, vinegar and sweeteners. The brand I prefer is Wan Ja Shan.

Pickled Ginger. Most notably used as a sushi condiment, pickled ginger, or *gari*, is thinly sliced ginger preserved in sweet vinegar or a vinegar-sugar solution. It's widely available in Asian food stores.

Sambal. A fiery, chilli-based condiment from Southeast Asia, the type I use, and which you're most likely to find, is *sambal oelek*. It's usually made from chillies, vinegar, sugar and salt, and is without other ingredients such as garlic and shrimp paste found in other sambal types.

Shoyu Ponzu. This thin citrus-based Japanese sauce with added soy or tamari sauce is also made with ingredients that can include mirin, rice vinegar, *katsobushi* (dried fermented tuna) and seaweed. I use a naturally brewed, wheat-free, tamari-based sauce made by Wan Ja Shan.

Soy Sauce. The indispensable Chinese and Japanese seasoning, soy sauce has been used for millennia. I call for naturally brewed standard or 'light' soy sauce, which is sometimes called 'thin', rather than the darker or thicker kinds. Soy sauce is made from a soya bean, flour and water mixture and should be naturally fermented or brewed rather than synthetically or chemically

produced. Look for 'naturally brewed' on the label and read ingredient listings. Avoid soy sauces that contain hydrolysed soya protein, corn syrup and caramel colour – a sure sign of an ersatz sauce. I use Japanese Kikkoman soy sauce as a standby, but I prefer an organic brand.

Sriracha. A Thai hot sauce made with chillies, garlic salt and vinegar, sriracha has the consistency of ketchup, and varies in heat, from super-hot to mild. Huy Fong, which comes in a squeeze bottle, is definitely on the hotter side of the spectrum, and this is the brand I commonly use.

Tamari . Sometimes confused with soy sauce, tamari is also soya bean-based, but it's darker and richer than ordinary soy sauce. I call for wheat-free tamari, which is sometimes labelled 'organic, wheat-free', which I prefer for its pure good taste. Check labels to assure yourself of wheat-free tamari. Wan Ja Shan is my brand of choice.

Thai Basil. Native to Southeast Asia, the plant has narrow leaves and purplish stems and a sweet liquorice taste with lemon undertones. I find its flavour more interesting than the ordinary kind; I also find that it retains its fragrance in cooking to a greater degree than sweet basil.

Togarashi. Japanese chillies that are available fresh or dried, and also dried and ground. The latter is required for the recipes in this book, and can be found in bottles in Asian food stores.

Vegetarian Oyster Sauce. Ordinary oyster sauce is a versatile Chinese ingredient made from cooked fresh oysters that are seasoned with soy sauce, salt and spices. Though its slightly fishy taste dissipates in cooking, some people would rather forgo oysters entirely. For them I recommend vegetarian oyster sauce, which is made from shiitake mushrooms rather than oysters – a sensible substitution, as both are umami-rich. I prefer the Wan Ja Shan brand.

Vegetarian Stir-Fry Sauce. Used as a flavouring finish for stir-fries, this sauce sometimes contains its own thickening agent and most contain soy sauce. I prefer the mushroom-based kind made by Wan Ja Shan.

OTHER INGREDIENTS

Chinese Sausages. Called *lap chong*, these small, thin dried sausages are made from pork or duck; the former is the kind you're most likely to find. *Lap chong* are sweetened and often steamed before using. Buy them in Chinese food stores or from some speciality meat shops or online suppliers.

Couscous. This staple of North African cuisine, a kind of pasta, is made from coarsely ground semolina mixed with water and then dried. Two types are available – the pre-steamed 'instant' kind and the traditional variety that must be steamed to cook to fluffiness. The traditional kind is used for recipes in this book. Couscous also comes in three grain sizes: coarse, medium and fine – medium is most typical – and in wholemeal versions. Buy couscous in packets or from Middle Eastern and health/natural food stores in bulk.

Minced Dark Turkey or Chicken Meat. If you can source this from a butcher's shop, or prepare your own, it makes a relatively low-fat and flavourful alternative to beef mince for burgers and meatloaf. Alternatively, use good-quality ready-prepared turkey or chicken mince.

Panko. Because these Japanese breadcrumbs are large and flat, they coat foods for frying and sautéeing better, resulting in delicately crunchy crusts. Panko is widely available in Asian food stores and many supermarkets.

Rice Flour. This gluten-free powdery flour is typically used for baking, but also makes a superior batter for coating seafood and vegetables for frying. Rice flour is widely available.

Seitan and Tempeh. Two versatile, protein-rich foods with firm chewy textures that are good substitutes for meat in stir-fries and other dishes, where they readily pick up flavours. Seitan is made from wheat gluten and is available in packages or tubs in the refrigerator section of health/natural and Asian food stores. Tempeh, a soya bean product, is also available in packages, fresh or frozen, from the same outlets.

Tea-Smoked Salmon. We make our own tea-smoked salmon at Blue Ginger, and so can you, but this wonderfully flavoured ingredient can also be bought.

Tofu. An ancient Chinese and Japanese product that's prepared from curdled soya milk in a process similar to cheese-making. It comes in extra-firm, firm, soft and silken styles, and is also available smoked. Silken tofu is the most delicate. Rich in protein, low in fat and cholesterol-free, tofu is extremely nutritious. Though sold fresh in water, it's most commonly available in packs or tubs. Refrigerate unused portions in the original container, or transfer to water and refresh daily.

TECHNIQUES AND OTHER MATTERS

Brining. I like to brine pork before cooking it (ditto chicken and turkey for Thanksgiving and Christmas) and recommend you do too. The process, which involves soaking meat or poultry in a solution of salt, water and sugar, enhances taste and maximises juiciness. It works because the brined item absorbs and retains the soaking liquid. Brining instructions appear in the respective recipes.

Food Sensitivities. To avoid potential allergic reactions, work smart. Always clean your chopping board and knife between chopping jobs. If, for example, I'm chopping nuts, I reflexively wash my board and knife before chopping another ingredient on it. Keeping your board and knife clean this way also avoids cross-contamination – the transfer of bacteria from raw ingredients to cooked ones. This is particularly important when you're having guests whose food sensitivities you – or they – may not know.

Heating the Pan. To minimise the possibility of sticking, all my recipes instruct that a pan used for browning be heated before adding oil. Following this method, the oil is in contact with the pan for less time and is thus less likely to break down – to become viscous and gummy and thus sticky. Even a trace of broken-down oil can contribute to sticking.

Making Rice. To make perfectly cooked rice every time, I recommend using a rice cooker, as millions of Asians do, with the added advantage that the cooked rice can be held hot in the cooker for up to 8 hours. For making white or brown rice, or a combination of the two, I

always use the 'Mt Fuji' method, which involves using your hand to determine how much water is needed in relation to the rice (see 50-50 White and Brown Rice for 4 Servings, below).

Organic Poultry and Meat. I always advise cooks to seek out meat and poultry that's certified organic – or is labelled in such a way to indicate that the animal has been humanely raised, without hormones or growth promotants, and on wholesome feed. As for poultry, I specify that the birds be free-range. Because of the care given to birds destined for the kosher table, I also recommend kosher chicken and meat products. If you can, buy meat and poultry that's been locally processed by small producers, which are usually more conscientious about animal welfare than mass-manufacturers. The pay-off for such choosiness is healthier, more flavourful eating.

Seasoning. My recipes call for frequent seasoning adjustments, as necessary – 'correcting' salt and pepper, and other seasonings, as you cook. This means tasting a dish frequently while cooking – repeated tasting is basic to ensuring a delicious result. Please understand that I don't advise overloading a dish with one seasoning or another, but rather bringing it to its maximum flavour potential through judicious seasoning adjustment.

Sustainable Tuna. I always recommend that cooks buy sustainable tuna, which comes from a fishery with practices that don't reduce the species' ability to maintain its population, and that don't negatively affect the food source of other species or damage their environment. Tuna should be caught by troll or 'pole and line' – using fishing pole and bait – rather than by long lines, which use baited hooks attached at intervals. There are other criteria for sustainable fishing. Always ask the person from whom you buy tuna where and how the fish was caught. If they don't know or you don't get a satisfying answer, shop elsewhere. For futher information go to goodfishguide.co.uk.

50-50 WHITE AND BROWN RICE FOR 4 SERVINGS

Rinse 275g brown long-grain rice and soak it in fresh cold water to cover for 1 hour. Transfer the rice to a medium saucepan.

Put 275g white long-grain rice in a large bowl in the sink. Rinse the rice by filling the bowl with cold water and stirring the rice with your hand. Drain and repeat until the water in the bowl is clean. Transfer the rice to the same saucepan.

Flatten the rice with your palm and without removing it, add water until it touches the highest knuckle of your middle finger. Cover and boil over high heat for 10 minutes. Lower the heat to medium and simmer for 30 minutes. Turn off the heat and let the rice stand, covered, to plump, for 20 minutes. Stir gently and serve.

Ming's Tip

To store cooked rice to be used for fried rice, spread it out in a thin layer on a clean baking sheet. Refrigerate, uncovered, overnight and break up any clumps before adding to a stir-fried rice recipe. If short on time, place the baking sheet in the freezer for 30 minutes, but check to make sure it doesn't freeze.

CHAPTER 1

Platters

Platters should invite sociability, and the ones here do just that. Placed on a coffee or buffet table, bar or kitchen counter, they bring people together. And many can be prepared ahead, frozen and finished before serving. That's social security in the freezer.

Party bites must be delicious. Crispy Vegetable Spring Rolls, which feature caramelised onions and crunchy carrots, and Prawn and Mango Summer Rolls – hot, sweet and cooling – make an instant impression. So do luscious Honey Crab Wontons and Pan-Fried Scallop Satays with Bacon and Black Bean Aioli, an update of the beloved bacon and scallop duo.

I like to surprise guests with novel presentations. Onion-Burger 'Hot Dogs' with Sweet Chilli Relish – hot dog-shaped burgers served in hot dog rolls – always delight. So does Wok-Stirred Tuna Poke on Sushi Rice, which are presented in Chinese spoons, and Parsnip Purée with Curry–Ginger Oil, offered in espresso cups. Smashed Prawn Shumai – prawn mousse dumplings that are flattened for manageability – invite happy nibbling.

I'm particularly proud of my Sushi Rolling Party, which offers four maki recipes that guests make and plate themselves. The rolling is lots of fun and, no matter how unchefly the result, everyone digs in. Another way that platters make good times happen.

Spring rolls are the perfect party food. Delicious and easily handled – you can cut them into bite-sized pieces – they invite happy munching. These fried vegetable rolls, which feature caramelised onions and grated carrot, also make a perfect counterpoint to meat- or seafood-based hors d'oeuvres.

I use lumpia to wrap these – Philippine wrappers that, I've found, make the crispest, most delicate spring rolls. You can find them at some Asian food stores. A final lettuce wrap adds more textural excitement.

CRISPY VEGETABLE SPRING ROLLS

MAKES 15

1 packet (about 250g) rice vermicelli or bean thread noodles

1 tablespoon rapeseed (canola) oil, plus extra for frying

2 large onions, sliced about 5mm thick

Sea salt and freshly ground black pepper

1 tablespoon finely chopped fresh ginger

1 tablespoon finely chopped garlic

1 butterhead lettuce, separated into leaves

120ml hoisin sauce

225g peeled carrots, grated

10–12 square lumpia wrappers

1 egg beaten with 1 tablespoon water, for egg wash

Leaves from 1 bunch mint

DIM SUM DIPPER

1 tablespoon sambal

3 tablespoons rice vinegar

2 tablespoons naturally brewed soy sauce

To Drink:

A Champagne or sparkling wine like Veuve Clicquot, or a Prosecco

1 Put the noodles in a large bowl and fill it with hot water to cover. When the noodles have softened, after about 15 minutes for rice vermicelli or 10 minutes for bean threads, drain and chop roughly. Weight out 210g noodles and set aside.

2 Heat a large sauté pan over a medium heat. Add the 1 tablespoon oil and swirl to coat the pan. When the oil is hot, add the onions. Season with salt and pepper and flip to incorporate, then add the ginger and garlic. Don't stir while you cook for about 5 minutes so that the onions can caramelise.

3 Meanwhile, make the dipper. In a small bowl, combine the sambal, vinegar and soy sauce, and set aside. Prepare the lettuce wrappers by picking out 10–12 large leaves from the inner third of the lettuce.

4 Flip the onions and cook for a further 5 minutes on the other side. Add the hoisin sauce to the caramelised onions and cook, stirring, for 1 minute. Transfer the mixture to a medium bowl, add the noodles and carrots, season with salt and pepper and stir to combine. Cool.

5 To make the rolls, place a wrapper on a work surface with a corner near you. Place 2 heaped tablespoons of the filling a little above the corner and bring the near corner of the wrapper over the filling to enclose it. Brush the edges with the egg wash, roll to the middle of the wrapper, fold in the sides and continue to roll. Rest the roll seam side down and repeat with the remaining wrappers and filling.

6 Fill a deep-fat fryer or medium heavy saucepan one-third full with oil. Over a high heat, bring to 190°C on a deep-frying thermometer. Gently drop half the rolls into the oil and fry for about 5 minutes until golden brown. Remove with a large mesh spoon and drain on kitchen paper. Repeat with the remaining rolls.

7 To serve, place a roll at the bottom of a lettuce leaf. Place 2 mint leaves on top and roll to enclose as you did previously. Transfer the rolls to a platter and serve with the dipper.

Ming's tip:

To make these in advance, fry the rolls for 3–4 minutes until pale gold, drain them and let them cool to room temperature. Transfer the rolls to resealable plastic bags and freeze for up to 2 weeks. When ready to serve, fry them again still frozen – be on guard for splattering as you add them to the oil – for about 2 minutes until golden, then transfer them to a colander. Leave for about 4 minutes to allow the heat to penetrate their interiors. Return the rolls to the fryer for about 1 minute to re-crisp, drain, wrap in the lettuce and serve.

I call these light, fresh-tasting rolls summer rolls because they feature basil, a herb I associate with that season. Mangoes, a warm-weather fruit, add tropical allure, and nicely accent the sweetness of the prawns. Sambal adds heat, which is 'cooled' by fresh mint. In other words, this dish is a party for your mouth. I like to wrap these in rice paper, but, for simplicity and even more freshness, you can use lettuce leaves instead.

PRAWN AND MANGO SUMMER ROLLS

MAKES 8

Sea salt

16 large raw prawns, peeled, deveined and halved lengthways

2 medium ripe mangoes, peeled, stoned, halved and sliced 3mm thick

Juice of 2 limes

1 tablespoon fish sauce

1 teaspoon sambal or hot sauce, or to taste

Freshly ground black pepper

8 rice paper wrappers or 8 butterhead lettuce leaves

Leaves from 1 bunch Thai basil or ordinary basil

1 Fill a large bowl with water and add ice cubes. Bring a large saucepan of salted water to the boil, add the prawns and blanch for about 30 seconds to 1 minute until they are just cooked through. Drain and transfer to the bowl of iced water to stop the cooking. Immediately drain the prawns and transfer to a medium bowl. Add the mangoes, lime juice, fish sauce and sambal, season with pepper and stir to combine.

2 Soften the rice paper wrappers, if using: Place one in a circular baking dish and cover with hot water. Soak for 15–30 seconds until just softened. Transfer the wrapper to a lint-free tea towel to drain, top with a second tea towel and blot dry. Transfer the rice paper to a flat surface, place 4 pieces of prawn from the filling across the centre of the wrapper and top with one-eighth of the filling. Top with 3 or 4 basil leaves and roll, folding in the sides halfway through. Alternatively, roll using lettuce leaves. Repeat with the remaining rice paper or lettuce leaves, prawns and filling.

3 Halve each roll on the diagonal and serve immediately.

Ming's tip:

These can prepared ahead of time and placed in a rectangular storage container. Cover the rolls with a damp tea towel, cover it with cling film, then snap on the lid. Refrigerate and bring to room temperature before serving.

Video tip:

Watch the video for my secret to using rice paper wrappers.

To Drink:

A New World Sauvignon Blanc, like Wither Hills, from New Zealand

I've based these on crab rangoon, the deep-fried, crab-filled dumplings of Chinese restaurant cooking. Often made with imitation crab and too much cream cheese, they can fall below the mark. Not, however, my super version, made with the best crab, a touch of honey, jicama for crunch and just enough cream cheese for richness. A perfect party nibble, these can be formed in advance and then stored in the fridge and fried just before serving.

HONEY CRAB WONTONS

MAKES ABOUT 40

450g cooked fresh white crabmeat

2 tablespoons runny honey

125g peeled jicama, diced

3 tablespoons thinly sliced chives

60g cream cheese, at room
   temperature

Sea salt and freshly ground
   black pepper

1 packet thin square wonton
   wrappers

1 egg beaten with 1 tablespoon
   water, for egg wash

Rapeseed (canola) oil for frying

1 In a medium bowl, combine the crabmeat, 1 tablespoon of the honey, the jicama, 2 tablespoons of the chives and the cream cheese. Season with salt and pepper and blend.

2 Place one wonton wrapper on a work surface with a corner nearest to you. Place a scant tablespoon of the filling in the centre of the wrapper, moisten the edges with the egg wash and fold the bottom half over the top to create a triangular dumpling. Bring the left and right sides under the dumpling, moisten the points with the egg wash and pinch together to seal. Repeat with the remaining wrappers and filling.

3 Fill a deep-fat fryer or medium heavy saucepan one-third full with oil. Over a high heat, bring to 180°C on a deep-frying thermometer. Add half the wontons and fry for about 2 minutes until golden brown. Remove with a large mesh spoon and drain on kitchen paper. Repeat with the remaining wontons.

4 Transfer to a platter, drizzle with the remaining 1 tablespoon honey, sprinkle with the remaining chives and serve.

Ming's tip:
Don't overfill the wontons or they won't seal properly.

Video tips:
Watch the video to see my simple technique for peeling and dicing jicama, and to learn how to form wontons.

To Drink:
An off-dry Semillon or a Fiano de Avellino like Feudi San Gregorio from Italy

Barbecued skewered food is irresistible. Satays – the snack-sized Indonesian version – also make terrific party bites, as they're easily handled as well as delicious. These satays feature chicken breasts, marinated first to ensure juiciness, and a basil purée garnish. I think of the purée as a quickly done pesto; it's a great flavouring 'drizzle' to keep in mind for garnishing soups or as a pasta sauce. For serving ease, the purée also eliminates the need to hand round a separate sauce.

BARBECUED GARLIC CHICKEN SATAYS
with Basil Purée

MAKES 18

2 tablespoons finely chopped garlic, plus 2 cloves, peeled, for the purée

3 tablespoons rapeseed (canola) oil, plus extra for brushing the barbecue rack, baking sheet or griddle pan

2 tablespoons naturally brewed soy sauce

Freshly ground black pepper

3 boneless, skinless chicken breasts (about 675g), see Tip

Sea salt

Leaves from 1 bunch basil

120ml extra-virgin olive oil

Banana leaf or shredded cabbage or iceberg lettuce

Eighteen 15–20cm wooden skewers

1 In a medium bowl, combine the 2 tablespoons garlic, 3 tablespoons of the rapeseed (canola) oil and the soy sauce. Season the marinade with pepper and stir.

2 Butterfly each chicken breast by placing it with the thin end nearest to you. With a palm resting on the breast, run a knife parallel to your work surface through the thickest side of the breast and open like a book. Cut each breast into 6 equal vertical strips. Add the strips to the marinade, turn to coat and refrigerate for 1–2 hours. Meanwhile, soak the skewers in a bowl of water for 1 hour.

3 Remove the chicken from the marinade and thread a skewer straight through each strip. Preheat an outdoor barbecue or indoor grill, or use a large griddle pan. If grilling, cover a baking sheet with foil and set the shelf in the middle position.

4 Fill a large bowl with water and add ice cubes. Bring a large saucepan of salted water to the boil. Add the basil and blanch for about 30 seconds to 1 minute until the leaves are bright green. Drain the basil in a large sieve and transfer the sieve with the leaves to the bowl of iced water. When the basil is cold, drain and squeeze the leaves to remove all the water. Transfer to a blender. Add the 2 garlic cloves to the blender and blend, drizzling in the olive oil to make a purée. Add 2 tablespoons water, or more, so that the mixture can be drizzled. Season with salt and pepper.

5 Brush the barbecue rack, baking sheet or griddle pan with rapeseed (canola) oil. Season the chicken with salt and pepper and barbecue or grill, or cook in the griddle pan, turning once, for 2–3 minutes per side until cooked through. Set aside.

6 Place the banana leaf or spread the cabbage or lettuce on a serving platter. Top with the satays, drizzle with the basil purée and serve.

To Drink:
A Rioja like Faustino VII

Ming's tip:

You can also use the chicken breast to make chicken fingers. I coat them with panko breadcumbs, which makes the most delicate crust.

Video tip:

Watch the video to learn how to butterfly chicken breasts.

I'm a golfing fiend. For a while, I spent as much time as I could golfing at the Olympic Club in San Francisco. One of its attractions, besides the course itself, was its signature dish, hot dog-shaped burgers served in hot dog buns, garnished with a fantastic chilli sauce. Here's my version, which makes another great party nibble. The burger shape is the same, but I've upped the ante by adding onions to the beef and making sure the sauce has an intense spicy-sweet tang. Serve this with your favourite chips.

ONION-BURGER 'HOT DOGS'
with Sweet Chilli Relish

MAKES 8

3 tablespoons rapeseed (canola) oil
2 large onions, finely chopped
Sea salt and freshly ground
    black pepper
1 tablespoon finely chopped garlic
1 large red pepper, finely chopped
1 tablespoon sambal or hot sauce,
    or to taste
2 tablespoons light agave syrup
    or runny honey
120ml rice vinegar
1 tablespoon cornflour mixed
    with 1 tablespoon cold water
900g beef mince
55g unsalted butter
8 hot dog rolls

1 Heat a large heavy frying pan over a medium heat. Add 1 tablespoon of the oil and swirl to coat the pan. When the oil is hot, add the onions, season with salt and pepper and brown, without stirring, for 5–6 minutes. Turn and brown for a further 3–4 minutes. Transfer half the onions to a large bowl and cool.

2 Meanwhile, add the garlic to the pan, season with salt and pepper and sauté, stirring, for 1 minute. Add the red pepper and sauté, stirring, for 30 seconds, then add the sambal and agave, stir and add the vinegar. Bring to a simmer, whisk in the cornflour mixture and simmer for about 30 seconds until the relish is thickened. Transfer to a bowl and cool to room temperature. Wipe out the pan.

3 Put the beef mince in a large bowl and add the reserved onions, season with salt and pepper and combine lightly. Very gently shape the beef mixture into 8 thick ovals the length of the rolls, and flatten the tops. Season with salt and pepper. Heat the frying pan over a medium-high heat, add the remaining 2 tablespoons oil and swirl to coat the pan. When the oil is hot, add the beef patties and cook, turning once, for about 4 minutes per side for medium-rare, 1 minute more per side for medium and 1 minute more per side for medium-well.

4 Meanwhile, heat half the butter in a medium pan over a medium-high heat. When the butter has melted, add half the hot dog rolls crumb side down and toast, moving them in the butter, for about 1 minute until brown and crisp. Repeat with the remaining butter and rolls.

5 Transfer the 'hot dogs' to the rolls and cover generously with the relish. Transfer to a platter and serve.

To Drink:

A Syrah blend like Arrogant Frog Croak Rotie Syrah Viognier from France

Ming's tips:

You can make the relish and store it overnight, refrigerated.

You can toast the rolls without butter in a toaster, toaster oven or under the grill, if you like.

Pork and rice-noodle salad, seasoned with lemongrass and served on lettuce, is a Vietnamese treat. My version, which features pork patties, has extra zing due to jalapeño heat, and makes a terrific party dish. The textural contrasts – slithery noodles, chewy meat, crisp lettuce – really make diners happy, including those from the younger generation.

LEMONGRASS PORK LETTUCE CUP

MAKES 8

1 small packet (about 200g) rice vermicelli

Juice of 1 lime

2 tablespoons fish sauce

1 bunch spring onions, white and green parts separated, thinly sliced

2 tablespoons rapeseed (canola) oil

1 tablespoon finely chopped fresh ginger

2 tablespoons finely chopped lemongrass (white part only)–see Tip, page 166

1 jalapeño chilli, finely chopped

Sea salt and freshly ground black pepper

450g pork mince

1 large head iceberg lettuce

1 Put the noodles in a medium bowl and fill it with hot water to cover. When the noodles have softened, after about 15 minutes, drain and weigh out 225g noodles. Return the noodles to the bowl and add the lime juice, fish sauce and spring onion greens, then toss and set aside.

2 Heat a medium heavy frying pan over a medium heat. Add 1 tablespoon of the oil and swirl to coat the pan. When the oil is hot, add the spring onion whites, ginger, lemongrass and jalapeño. Sauté, stirring, for about 2 minutes until the vegetables are soft. Transfer to a medium bowl and cool. Wipe out the pan.

3 Add the pork mince to the bowl, season with salt and pepper and mix lightly. With wet hands, form 8 oval patties about 1cm thick. Heat the pan over a medium-high heat, add the remaining 1 tablespoon oil and swirl to coat the pan. When the oil is hot, add the pork patties and cook until browned, turning once, for 3–4 minutes per side.

4 Pick 8 nice lettuce cups from a third of the way into your iceberg head. Place one piece of lettuce on your work surface. Top with one-eighth of the noodle salad and a patty. Repeat with the remaining lettuce, salad and patties. Transfer to a platter, garnish with the spring onion greens and serve.

To Drink:
An unoaked Chardonnay

Video tip:
Watch the video to see me demonstrate how to finely chop lemongrass.

Anyone who pooh-poohs aubergine – and I've met too many who do – hasn't tasted aubergine caviar my way. Smoky and seriously garlic-flavoured, it's served with crisps made from pitta bread that's first sprinkled with curry powder – a terrific combination, to say the least. I usually serve the caviar as a dip, surrounded by the crisps, but you can also plate the crisps and dollop the caviar on them. The recipe makes a good quantity of caviar, but having extra in the fridge for later enjoyment isn't a problem, believe me.

ROASTED AUBERGINE CAVIAR
with Curry Pitta Crisps

MAKES 24 CRISPS AND 950ML CAVIAR

2 large aubergines
3 small or 2 large heads garlic
3 tablespoons extra-virgin olive
  oil, plus extra for drizzling and
  brushing
Sea salt and freshly ground
  black pepper
4 wholemeal pitta breads
1 tablespoon curry powder
1 bunch spring onions, white and
  green parts separated, thinly sliced
120ml balsamic vinegar

1 Preheat the oven to 200°C/fan 180°C/Gas Mark 6. Put the aubergines on a large baking tray. Cut the tops off the garlic heads, drizzle with oil, season with salt and pepper and wrap each in foil. Transfer to the baking tray and roast the aubergines and garlic for about 1 hour until soft. Cool.

2 Lower the oven temperature to 175°C/fan 155°C/Gas Mark 4. Brush both sides of each pitta bread lightly with oil, sprinkle with the curry powder and season with salt. Halve each bread vertically, then cut each half into thirds. Place the crisps on a baking sheet and bake for about 15 to 20 minutes until crisp, turning once.

3 When the aubergine can be handled, halve the aubergines and scoop the flesh into a food processor. Squeeze the garlic from the cloves into the processor, add the spring onion whites, season with salt and pepper and purée, drizzling in the 3 tablespoons oil. Adjust the seasoning and transfer the caviar to a serving bowl.

4 In a small non-reactive saucepan, bring the vinegar to the boil. Lower the heat and simmer for 2–3 minutes until the vinegar is reduced to a syrupy consistency.

5 Place the caviar in a bowl. Sprinkle with the spring onion greens and surround with the crisps. Drizzle the syrup over the caviar and crisps and serve.

Ming's tip:
The caviar also makes a great filling for ravioli made with wonton wrappers. You can boil or pan-sear them.

To Drink:
A French Pinot Noir like Louis Latour Domaine de Valmossine

SUSHI ROLLING PARTY

A sushi rolling party is fun for everyone. Guests really get into the easily mastered process of making maki, then enjoy the result of everyone's efforts, no matter how non-pro.

The host should prepare the sushi rice beforehand and keep it warm in a temperature-holding container like the Igloo sushi restaurants favour or in a glass or metal bowl covered with cling film, then foil. Bring the rice to your rolling area – a large table or kitchen island, for example.

Do your *mise en place* – prep all the recipes you'll use up to the point of rolling, including the water-vinegar mixture used for making the maki and handrolls. Place all ingredients in suitable dishes or small bowls that can be brought to the rolling area.

I like to have a rolling mat for each person – they're inexpensive – but you can certainly get away with fewer, depending on the number of guests. You'll also want to have slicing knives on hand to cut the rolls – straight across into eight pieces, on the bias into thirds or any way you like – and a platter or platters lined with banana leaves or shredded cabbage or shredded iceberg lettuce for serving the sushi. Dishes of soy sauce, wasabi and pickled ginger, the traditional sushi condiments, should also be on hand.

When everyone has gathered, demonstrate the rolling process – and your guests are in business.

To Drink:
A Riesling blend like Cameron Hughes Lot 259 for all but the fennel chicken maki. For it, a Pinot Noir, like Cloudline, from Oregon, and/or Botani Moscatel from Spain

You will need to make two batches of this recipe if you're planning a full party with all four maki recipes. One batch will get you through two maki recipes, and if you halve this, you can make a party for one maki roll.

SUSHI RICE

MAKES ABOUT 3.2KG

1 Place 1.6kg short-grain sushi rice in a bowl or rice-cooker insert and add water to cover it generously. Swish the rice in a single direction to rinse off residual starch. Drain, refill the bowl or insert and swish again. Rinse and repeat until the water is clear.

2 Drain the rice and, if not using a rice cooker, transfer it to a medium saucepan with a tight lid. If using a rice cooker, dry the outside of the insert and place it in the cooker. Flatten the rice with a palm and, without removing your hand, add water until it just touches the highest knuckle of your middle finger. Cover the pan and bring the water to the boil over a high heat – 10–15 minutes. Reduce the heat to medium and simmer for 30 minutes. Turn off the heat and leave the rice to stand for 20 minutes, covered, to plump. If using a rice cooker, turn it on.

3 Meanwhile, in a small non-reactive saucepan, combine 240ml rice wine vinegar, 60ml mirin and 100g granulated sugar and heat for about 5 minutes until hot; don't allow the mixture to boil. Keep hot.

4 Invert the rice into a large stainless-steel or wooden bowl. (Don't include any browned bits that may have formed on the base of the pan.) Using a wooden or rubber spatula, gently fold half the vinegar mixture into the rice using a light, lifting motion to avoid mashing the rice. Taste; the rice should have a pleasingly sweet-acidic edge. If not, fold in more of the vinegar mixture.

5 Dampen a clean tea towel. With your hands, gently push the rice together to form a loose mound. Cover the towel and allow the rice to rest for 20 minutes to develop its flavour. Store any leftovers in the refrigerator for up to 3 days.

Tuna is among the most popular sushi ingredients. Here, top-grade tuna is tossed in a chilli-honey mixture, then made into deliciously hot-sweet rolls.

SPICY TUNA MAKI

MAKES 8 ROLLS

- 1 serrano chilli, finely chopped, or to taste
- 1 tablespoon runny honey
- 1 teaspoon naturally brewed soy sauce, plus extra for serving
- 1 tablespoon thinly sliced chives
- 225g sashimi-grade tuna, preferably big-eye or yellowfin, diced
- Sea salt and freshly ground black pepper

- 1 tablespoon rice vinegar mixed with 240ml water, for rolling
- 1.6kg cooked Sushi Rice (opposite)
- 8 toasted nori sheets, halved lengthways

- Naturally brewed soy sauce
- Wasabi
- Sliced pickled ginger

1 In a medium bowl, combine the chilli, honey, soy sauce, chives and tuna. Season with salt and pepper and gently mix.

2 To roll the sushi, have the vinegar-water mixture and sushi rice handy. Place a half sheet of the nori vertically on a work surface, shiny side down. With wet hands, pat 200g of the rice evenly over the bottom half of the nori. Top the bottom third of the rice with 3 teaspoons of the tuna mixture. To roll, lift the mat, compressing it against the filling as you roll the bottom edge in on itself. Continue rolling towards the top edge until only 5mm of the nori remains unrolled. Moisten your finger in the water, wet the edge of the nori and press the mat to seal the roll. Set the roll aside, seam side down, and repeat.

3 With a sharp knife, slice each roll as preferred (see photo on page 30). Transfer to a platter and serve with the soy sauce, wasabi and pickled ginger.

This delicious roll features buttery smoked salmon and tart cucumber, a dynamite combo. Guests should make the salmon and cucumber logs before rolling.

SMOKED SALMON AND CUCUMBER MAKI

MAKES 8 ROLLS

- 8 large or 16 small slices smoked salmon, preferably tea-smoked
- 1 cucumber, cut into 5mm x 20cm strips, or as long as the nori
- 1 tablespoon rice vinegar mixed with 240ml water, for rolling

- 1.6kg cooked Sushi Rice (opposite)
- 8 toasted nori sheets, halved lengthways

- Naturally brewed soy sauce
- Wasabi
- Sliced pickled ginger

1 Place 1 large or 2 small slightly overlapping slices of salmon on a work surface with a wide side near you. Place 2 cucumber strips a little above the near side of the salmon. Bring the near side of the salmon over the cucumber to enclose it, and roll to form a log. Transfer to a large plate and repeat.

2 To roll the sushi, have the vinegar-water mixture and sushi rice handy. Place a sheet of nori shiny side down on a sushi mat with one long edge towards you. With wet hands, pat 200g of the rice evenly over the bottom half of the nori. Place a salmon roll on the bottom third of the rice. Continue as above.

The almost creamy texture of avocado is one of the best things on the planet, I think. This simple but delicious roll features it, plus the flavours of lime, a touch of shallot and togarashi, for heat.

AVOCADO-LIME MAKI

MAKES 8 ROLLS

2 ripe avocados, cut into long
  5mm-wide strips
Pinch of sea salt
1–3 pinches of togarashi, to taste
Juice of 1 lime
1 shallot, thinly sliced
16 shiso leaves (optional)
1 tablespoon rice vinegar mixed
  with 240ml water, for rolling
1.6kg cooked Sushi Rice (page 32)
8 toasted nori sheets

Naturally brewed soy sauce
Wasabi
Sliced pickled ginger

1 Put the avocados in a medium bowl and season with the salt and togarashi. Add the lime juice and shallot and toss gently to avoid mashing the avocado.

2 To roll the sushi, have the vinegar-water mixture and sushi rice handy. Place a sheet of nori shiny side down on a sushi mat with one long edge towards you. With wet hands, pat 200g of the rice evenly over the bottom half of the nori.

3 Lay a few shallot slices, 2 shiso leaves, if using, and 3 or 4 of the avocado strips over the bottom third of the rice. To roll, lift the mat, compressing it against the filling as you roll the bottom edge in on itself. Continue rolling towards the top edge until only 5mm of the nori remains unrolled. Moisten your finger in the water-vinegar mixture, wet the edge of the nori and press the mat to seal the roll. Set the roll aside, seam side down, and repeat with the remaining nori and filling.

4 With a sharp knife, slice each roll as preferred (see photo on page 30). Transfer the pieces to a platter and serve with the soy sauce, wasabi and pickled ginger.

This delicious roll features seared chicken breasts that have been rubbed with a spicy fennel-flavoured mixture. If possible, have your guests prepare and cook the chicken, as the rolls are extra-super when the chicken in them is still hot.

FENNEL AND GARLIC CHICKEN MAKI

MAKES 8 ROLLS

1 tablespoon natural garlic powder

1 teaspoon cayenne or chilli powder, or to taste

1 teaspoon paprika

1 tablespoon fennel seeds, coarsely crushed

65g plain flour

2 bonless, skinless chicken breasts (about 450g), cut lengthways into 5mm-thick strips

Sea salt and freshly ground black pepper

2 large eggs

60g panko breadcrumbs

2 tablespoons rapeseed (canola) oil

1 bunch spring onions, white and green parts, cut into 5cm lengths

1 red pepper, cut into 5mm-wide strips

1 tablespoon rice vinegar mixed with 240ml water, for rolling

1.6kg cooked Sushi Rice (page 32)

8 toasted nori sheets

Naturally brewed soy sauce
Wasabi
Sliced pickled ginger

1 Line a large plate with kitchen paper. In a small bowl, combine the garlic powder, cayenne, paprika, fennel and flour. Transfer to a shallow dish. Season the chicken with salt and pepper.

2 Put the eggs and panko in 2 other shallow dishes. Beat the eggs with 1 tablespoon water until well combined. Dredge the chicken in the flour mixture, dip in the egg and drain the excess, then dredge in the panko. Transfer to a plate.

3 Heat a medium frying pan over a medium heat. Add the oil and swirl to coat the pan. When the oil is hot, add the chicken and sauté, turning once, for 3–4 minutes per side until golden and cooked through. Transfer the chicken to the plate. Wipe out the pan, add the spring onions and red pepper and sauté over a medium-high heat for 2–3 minutes until the vegetables have softened slightly. Transfer to a plate.

4 To roll the sushi, have the vinegar-water mixture and sushi rice handy. Place a sheet of nori shiny side down on a sushi mat with one long edge towards you. With wet hands, pat 200g of the rice evenly over the bottom half of the nori.

5 Cover the rice with one-eighth of the chicken and top with one-eighth of the spring onion mixture. To roll, lift the mat, compressing it against the filling as you roll the bottom edge in on itself. Continue rolling towards the top edge until only 5mm of the nori remains unrolled. Moisten your finger in the water, wet the edge of the nori and press the mat to seal the roll. Set the roll aside, seam side down, and repeat with the remaining nori and filling.

6 With a sharp knife, slice each roll as preferred (see photo on page 30). Transfer to a platter and serve with the soy sauce, wasabi and pickled ginger.

This dish began with a near-disaster. I was making shumai for a TY KU Sake party, held in Aspen, Colorado. As the guests were arriving I realised that the water I was going to cook the dumplings in wasn't going to boil at our high altitude. What to do? I grabbed a paella pan, put it on the grill and added oil. I smashed – flattened – the shumai with a wet palm, then sautéed them until golden and crisp. The result, with its great textural play, was better than the original. These have a prawn mousse filling that's deluxe but easy to do. They make a fantastic party nibble, but I think you'll want to serve them as a first course, too.

SMASHED PRAWN SHUMAI

MAKES 20

450g large raw prawns, peeled and deveined

2 large eggs

115g unsalted butter, chilled and diced

1 teaspoon truffle oil (optional)

Sea salt and freshly ground white pepper

16 thin square wonton wrappers

1 bunch spring onions, white and green parts separated and thinly sliced, 2 tablespoons of the greens reserved for garnish

2 tablespoons sesame seeds

4 tablespoons rapeseed (canola) oil

1 In a food processor, combine the prawn and eggs and process until almost smooth. Add the butter and truffle oil, if using, season with salt and white pepper and pulse until the butter is incorporated but still visible in small pieces. Test a small amount for seasoning by microwaving it at high power for 10–15 seconds, or by sautéeing it in a little oil in a small pan. Adjust the seasoning if necessary. Use or place in a container, cover and store refrigerated for up to 2 days.

2 To form the shumai, have a bowl of water handy. Hold a wonton wrapper in the palm of your non-dominant hand. Cup the hand and place 1 heaped tablespoon of the mousse in the centre of the wrapper. Bring the wrapper up around the filling, pressing it to adhere to the filling and pleating as you go. Continue around the filling. There will be 6–8 pleats and the filling will be exposed. Tap the dumpling against the work surface to flatten the base. Repeat with the remaining wrappers and filling.

3 Put the spring onions on a platter. Add the sesame seeds and combine. With a wet palm, press down on the shumai, flattening them to a thickness of about 1cm. Press the 'open' top side of the shumai into the spring onion mixture.

4 Line a large plate with kitchen paper. Heat a large frying pan over a medium heat. Add 2 tablespoons of the oil and swirl to coat the pan. When the oil is hot, carefully add half the shumai to the pan coated side down and cook until golden, turning once, for 1½–2 minutes per side. The tip of a paring knife, when inserted in the shumai, should emerge hot. Transfer the shumai to the kitchen paper to drain. Cook the remaining shumai with the remaining 2 tablespoons oil. Transfer to a platter, sprinkle with the reserved spring onion greens and serve.

To Drink:

A smooth, fruity white wine, like Teruzzi & Puthod Terre di Tufi, from Italy

I love halibut when it's perfectly cooked – and this recipe ensures just that. Enriched with olive oil and flavoured with fennel, fresh halibut makes a luscious shumai filling. If you can find fennel pollen – yes, dried pollen from fennel plants – for the filling, by all means use it. It's intensely fennel-y *and* intriguingly sweet. These tempting dumplings are equally delicious as a party offering or first course.

STEAMED HALIBUT FENNEL SHUMAI

MAKES 24

1 tablespoon fennel pollen or
    fennel seeds
4 tablespoons extra-virgin olive oil
1 large onion, finely chopped
1 large fennel bulb, halved, cored
    and diced, fronds reserved
    for garnish
Sea salt and freshly ground
    black pepper
450g skinless halibut, preferably
    centre cut, cut into 2.5cm chunks
2 large eggs
24 thin square wonton wrappers

1 If using fennel seeds, place them in a dry medium pan over a medium heat and toast, tossing constantly, for 3–4 minutes until just beginning to smoke lightly. Immediately transfer the seeds to a rimmed plate and set aside.

2 Heat a large sauté pan over a medium-high heat. Add 1 tablespoon of the oil and swirl to coat the pan. When the oil is hot, add the onion and fresh fennel and sauté, stirring, for about 8 minutes until the onion is caramelised. Season with salt and pepper and transfer to a medium bowl. Cool.

3 Meanwhile, in a food processor combine the halibut, eggs and remaining 2 tablespoons oil and pulse until well combined. Season with salt and pepper. Test a small amount for seasoning by microwaving it at high power for 10–15 seconds, or by sautéeing it in a little oil in a small pan. Adjust the seasoning if necessary. Transfer the mousse to a medium bowl, add the fennel–onion mixture and fold together to combine.

4 To form the shumai, hold a wonton wrapper in the palm of your non-dominant hand. Cup the hand and place 1 heaped tablespoon of the mousse in the centre of the wrapper. Bring the wrapper up around the filling, pressing it to adhere to the filling and pleating as you go. Continue around the filling. There will be 6–8 pleats and the filling will be exposed. Tap the dumpling against the work surface to flatten the base. Repeat with the remaining wrappers and filling.

5 Set up a steamer. If using a stainless-steel steamer, spray with non-stick cooking spray; if using a bamboo basket, line one or more compartments with a banana leaf, shredded cabbage or baking paper. When the water boils, working in batches if necessary, add the shumai to the steamer tray. Sprinkle the fennel pollen or toasted fennel seeds on the shumai. Steam for about 5 minutes until the filling is cooked through, or the tip of a paring knife inserted into the shumai comes out clean and feels hot.

To Drink:
A Chardonnay like Montes Alpha

6 Transfer the shumai to a platter. Garnish with the fennel fronds and serve.

Everyone loves scallops and bacon. The salty smokiness of the bacon perfectly showcases the scallops' sweetness. Here, skewered, sautéed scallops are garnished with black bean mayo and crumbled bacon, a fabulous match-up. The scallops are threaded onto half skewers and make perfect, easily handled bites.

PAN-FRIED SCALLOP SATAYS
with Bacon and Black Bean Aioli

MAKES 12

36 cleaned scallops, corals removed
6 thick rashers bacon
1 tablespoon finely chopped garlic
1 tablespoon chopped fermented
  black beans
1 bunch spring onions, white and
  green parts separated, thinly
  sliced, 1 tablespoon of the greens
  reserved for garnish
Sea salt and freshly ground
  black pepper
2 egg yolks from large eggs, cold
1 tablespoon Dijon mustard
240ml plus 1 tablespoon extra-virgin
  oil or more if needed
Juice of ½ lemon
6 x 20cm wooden skewers, or
  12 smaller ones

1 Using heavy kitchen scissors, halve the 20cm skewers, if using. Transfer to a bowl of water and soak for about 1 hour.

2 Skewer 3 scallops and arrange them near the top of each skewer. Refrigerate if not using immediately.

3 Meanwhile, cover a large plate with kitchen paper. Heat a large cast-iron frying pan or sauté pan over a medium-high heat, add the bacon and sauté, turning as needed, for about 4 minutes until crisp. Transfer to the kitchen paper to drain. Discard half the bacon fat from the pan. Chop the bacon and transfer to a dish.

4 Return the pan to a medium heat. Add the garlic, black beans and spring onions and sauté, stirring, for about 1 minute until the vegetables are soft. Season with salt and pepper and transfer to a plate to cool. Wipe out the pan.

5 To make the mayonnaise, place the egg yolks, mustard and 240ml oil in a measuring jug and season with salt and pepper. Using an immersion blender, process until an emulsion forms, or prepare in a standard blender. Transfer the aioli to a small bowl and stir in the black bean mixture. Add the lemon juice and adjust the seasoning, if necessary. (If not serving right away, refrigerate.)

6 Season the scallops with salt and pepper. Heat the pan over a medium-high heat, add the 1 tablespoon oil and swirl to coat the pan. When the oil is hot, working in batches if necessary with additional oil, sauté the scallops, turning once, for 30 seconds per side until just cooked through. Transfer to a platter or plates, top with the aioli, garnish with the bacon and reserved spring onion greens and serve.

Ming's tips:

If you don't feel like making your own mayo, you can use a best-quality, rapeseed (canola) oil-based brand.

If you can find small skewers, use them instead of halving the larger kind.

To Drink:

A white Rhone blend like JL Columbo Les Abeilles Côte de Rhone Blanc

It's amazing how popular goat's cheese has become, and with reason. Besides its great taste, it's healthier than many other natural cheeses. It also pairs beautifully with earthy shiitakes, as in these bites. The crostini are easily made and are perfect for entertaining. I prefer to make them with a wholemeal baguette, but feel free to use the ordinary kind, if you like.

SHIITAKE AND GOAT'S CHEESE CROSTINI

MAKES ABOUT 20

1 baguette, preferably wholemeal, sliced into 5mm-thick rounds

2 tablespoons extra-virgin olive oil, plus extra for brushing

Sea salt and freshly ground black pepper

2 tablespoons finely chopped garlic

225g large shiitake mushrooms, stalks removed, sliced 5mm thick

120ml red wine

1 bunch chives, thinly sliced, a handful left whole for garnish

20 basil leaves

1 x 280g log goat's cheese, cut into 5mm-thick slices

1 Preheat the oven to 180°C/fan 160°C/Gas Mark 4. Place the bread rounds on a baking sheet, brush the tops with oil and season lightly with salt and pepper. Bake oiled side up for 10–12 minutes until golden. Remove from the oven, flip the rounds and set aside. Turn the oven to grill function, or preheat the grill.

2 Heat a large frying pan over a medium heat. Add 1 tablespoon of the oil and swirl to coat the pan. When the oil is hot, add the garlic and sauté, stirring, for 1 minute. Add the shiitakes, season with salt and pepper and sauté, stirring, for 2–3 minutes until softened. Add the wine to deglaze the pan and cook for 1–2 minutes until evaporated. Remove from the heat, add the chives and stir to combine.

3 To make the crostini, top each bread round with a basil leaf, some of the shiitake mixture and a slice of cheese. Drizzle with the remaining 1 tablespoon oil and season with pepper. Grill on the middle shelf of the grill for 1½–2 minutes just until the cheese becomes warm. Scatter the whole chives on a platter or plates, add the crostini and serve immediately.

Ming's tip:

The easiest way to cut the cheese into rounds is to use a piece of fishing line or waxed unflavoured dental floss, stretched taut. Alternatively, you can use a thin-bladed knife dipped into hot water.

Video tip:

Watch the video for my secret to cutting goat's cheese.

To Drink:

A French Pinot Noir like Arrogant Frog

I didn't invent the perfect combination of pears and gorgonzola, but their affinity did inspire the filling for these great quesadillas. Another great party nibble, they're made with mu shu wrappers, whose thinness makes them more delicate than the usual tortilla-wrapped kind. The gorgonzola doesn't melt, so count it as a textural as well as a flavour element in the quesadillas. Spanish ham – you can also use proscuitto – adds class of its own.

GORGONZOLA AND GINGERED PEAR
'Quesadillas'

MAKES 8

4 just-ripe Conference pears
Juice of 1 lime
1 tablespoon finely chopped fresh
  ginger
225g gorgonzola cheese, crumbled
8 mu shu wrappers
8 thin slices Jamón ham or proscuitto
Rapeseed (canola) oil

1 Peel, halve and core the pears. Dice, transfer to a medium bowl and add the lime juice, ginger and gorgonzola. Stir gently.

2 Lay the wrappers flat on your work surface. Lay 1 or 2 slices of ham on the bottom half of each wrapper and top with the pear mixture. Fold the wrappers in half to make a half-moon shape.

3 Working in batches, and using 1 tablespoon oil for each, heat the oil in the pan over a medium heat, swirling to coat the pan. When the oil is hot, carefully add as many quesadillas as will fit comfortably and cook for about 2 minutes until browned. With a large spatula, turn the quesadillas and brown the other side – about 2 minutes. Slice the quesadillas into 3 wedges each, transfer to a platter and serve.

Ming's tip:
If you can't get mu shu wrappers, available at some Asian food stores, you can use traditional flour tortillas instead.

Video tip:
Watch the video to learn my simple technique for perfectly dicing pears.

To Drink:
A Pinot Grigio like Kris or Alta Luna

As many people know, poke is a Hawaiian dish using cubed fish, raw or cooked. This cross-cultural poke, a simplified version of a Blue Ginger signature dish, features best-quality, stir-fried tuna cubes served on sushi rice in inexpensive Chinese spoons. People love this presentation, but you can use large tablespoons if you like, or eliminate the rice and serve the poke in a bowl as a 'dip' with crisps. You could also use salmon or halibut instead of the tuna, but whichever fish you choose, it must be top grade.

WOK-STIRRED TUNA POKE
on Sushi Rice

MAKES 30

1 tablespoon sesame seeds

2 bunches spring onions, white and green parts separated, whites and half the greens cut into 5mm-thick slices, the remaining greens thinly sliced

2 tablespoons finely chopped fresh ginger

60ml naturally brewed soy sauce

2 tablespoons runny honey

2 teaspoons toasted sesame oil

Freshly ground black pepper

450g centre-cut yellowfin tuna, cut into 1cm dice

1 tablespoon rapeseed (canola) oil

600g freshly cooked Sushi Rice (page 32)

Zest and juice of 1 lemon

30 Chinese spoons for serving

1 Put the sesame seeds in a dry wok over a medium heat and toast, tossing constantly, for about 30 seconds until golden. Immediately transfer the seeds to a rimmed plate and set aside.

2 In a medium bowl, combine the spring onion whites and the 5mm-sliced greens, the ginger, soy sauce, honey and sesame oil. Season with pepper and stir. Add the tuna, stir gently and transfer to the fridge to marinate for about 15 minutes. Drain the tuna of excess marinade.

3 Heat a wok or medium sauté pan over a high heat. Add the rapeseed (canola) oil and swirl to coat the pan. When the oil is hot, add the tuna and stir-fry for about 1 minute until rare, or about 3 minutes if you prefer the tuna cooked through. Transfer to a plate.

4 Fill each spoon with a small quantity of rice. Top with the tuna and sprinkle with the lemon zest and juice. Garnish with the sesame seeds and thinly sliced spring onion greens, and serve.

Ming's tip:
I give instructions for toasting sesame seeds, but you can also buy them already toasted if you like.

Video tip:
Watch the video to learn the best technique for cutting the fresh tuna.

To Drink:
A Champagne like Saint Hilaire Blanc de Blanc

This is an awesome treatment of the usually humble parsnip. The vegetable is transformed into a suave purée that's garnished with curry–ginger oil and served in espresso cups, a festive presentation. The recipe makes enough purée to have on its own as a soup the next day; any leftover curry–ginger oil can be stored and used for making a deliciously spicy vinaigrette or for sautéeing scallops, among other uses.

PARSNIP PURÉE
with Curry–Ginger Oil

MAKES 16

CURRY–GINGER OIL

20g Madras curry powder

500ml grapeseed or rapeseed (canola) oil

35g peeled fresh ginger, finely chopped

PARSNIP PURÉE

1 tablespoon rapeseed (canola) oil

1 large onion, roughly chopped

Cloves from 1 head garlic, smashed with the flat of a knife

6 large parsnips, peeled and roughly chopped

Sea salt and freshly ground black pepper

1 litre fresh chicken stock or low-sodium bought

25g unsalted butter

2 tablespoons thinly sliced chives

1 Four hours in advance, or the day before, make the curry–ginger oil. In a large heavy saucepan, heat the curry powder over a medium-high heat, stirring, for 30 seconds–1 minute until toasted. Add the oil and heat. When the oil is hot, add the ginger and cook for about 30 seconds until it sizzles. Remove from the heat, allow the oil to cool slightly, then transfer to a glass jar. Allow the mixture to stand for about 4 hours until the oil and curry powder have separated completely. (Store in the refrigerator for at least 1 month if not using immediately.)

2 Make the parsnip purée. Heat a large saucepan over a medium heat. Add the oil and swirl to coat the pan. When the oil is hot, add the onion and garlic and sauté, stirring, for 3–4 minutes until caramelised. Add the parsnips and sauté, stirring, for 2 minutes. Season with salt and pepper, add the stock and bring to a simmer. Cook for 20–25 minutes until the parsnips are tender and the liquid has reduced by one-third. Working in batches if necessary, transfer to a blender and purée on the lowest speed. Add the butter and purée on high. Adjust the seasoning if necessary.

3 Transfer the purée to warmed espresso or other serving cups (see the Tip). Drizzle with the curry–ginger oil, garnish with the chives and serve.

Ming's tip:

To heat the espresso cups for serving, put them in the sink and pour boiling water over them. Dry and use.

Video tip:

Watch the video for my simple roll-cutting technique for parsnips.

To Drink:

A Sauvignon Blanc

CHAPTER 2

Salads and Soups

When I think salads and soups, I think meals. Credit that to my French culinary training, which introduced me to tantalising main-dish salads and unique meal-in-one soups. Salads and soups, individually or together, make great lunches and dinners.

The salads here are all-occasion. Chicken Salad Chinoise, which pairs roast chicken with a tempting lettuce array, is perfect party fare. Miso-Shallot Prawn Frisée Salad, an East-West blend that features miso–ponzu dressing; basil-brightened Wok-Stirred Vegetables and Rice Noodle Salad; and light but luscious Salmon Salad with Shallot–Orange Vinaigrette all work perfectly for guests and family alike. Want to be the hit of someone else's party? Most of the salads can be prepared ahead for, say, pot-luck suppers, tossed with their vinaigrettes at the last minute and served.

Soups are meant to comfort. Quinoa and Tomato Soup starts with a beloved favourite – tomato soup – and includes the grain for hearty depth; Garlic–Ginger Sweet Potato Soup takes my favourite spud to a new and wonderfully satisfying height. I've tipped soups wholly into the rib-sticking zone with Chilli Miso Pork Stew and Best 3-Meat Chilli, which features turkey, pork and lamb mince, as well as black beans. Sambal Prawn Gumbo, which also includes Chinese sausage, is a spicy 'surf and turf' meal that's also great for company. And simplicity is key: all the soups are one-pot dishes, so they're easier on the cook. Whether soup or salad, the dishes here make the meal, in every sense.

This super salad, perfect for entertaining, was inspired by the popular chicken salad served by my friend Wolfgang Puck at his restaurant Chinois. My version offers two kinds of lettuce and grated carrots as well as sliced cabbage, and features a light vinaigrette that balances hot Chinese mustard with a touch of honey. Added too are cashews and crisped chicken skin. I can't think of anything better to serve as the centrepiece of a summer meal – or, really, at any time of year when you want something light *and* satisfying.

CHICKEN SALAD CHINOISE

SERVES 4–6

60g sea salt for brining,
plus extra for seasoning
65g granulated sugar
1 x 1.8–2.25kg chicken
1 tablespoon rapeseed (canola) oil
Freshly ground black pepper

VINAIGRETTE

1 large shallot, roughly chopped
2 tablespoons Dijon mustard
3 tablespoons Chinese hot mustard
powder
180ml rice vinegar
1½ tablespoons naturally brewed
soy sauce
3 tablespoons runny honey
2 tablespoons toasted sesame oil
Pinch of salt and freshly ground
black pepper
180ml groundnut or rapeseed (canola)
oil

1 cos lettuce, tough outer leaves
removed, cored, halved and cut
widthways into 2.5cm pieces
½ small head Chinese leaf, quartered
and thinly sliced
½ small red cabbage, halved,
cored and thinly sliced

1 Twelve to twenty-four hours in advance, brine the chicken. In a bowl large enough to hold the chicken and brine, combine the 60g salt, the sugar and about 1.9–2.4 litres water. Stir to dissolve the salt and sugar, then add the chicken. If the chicken isn't covered, add more water. Refrigerate.

2 Preheat the oven to 240°C/fan 220°C/Gas Mark 9. Rinse the chicken well and pat dry inside and out. Coat inside and out with the 1 tablespoon rapeseed (canola) oil, and season inside and out with salt and pepper. Place the chicken on a rack in a roasting pan breast side up and roast for 15–25 minutes until brown. Lower the oven temperature to 180°C/fan 160°C/Gas Mark 4 and roast for about 30 minutes until cooked through, or until a meat thermometer inserted into the thickest part of the thigh reads 70°C. (Don't turn off the oven.) Transfer the chicken to a plate and, when cool enough to handle, remove the skin and transfer to a small baking dish. Pull the meat from the bones, tearing into long shreds, season with salt and pepper and set aside. Decrease the oven to 120°C/fan 100°C/Gas Mark ½, return the skin to the oven and roast for 10–12 minutes until crisp, stirring occasionally. Slice the skin into 5mm-wide strips, transfer to a plate and set aside.

3 Meanwhile, make the vinaigrette. In a blender, combine the shallot, mustards, vinegar, soy sauce, honey and sesame oil, season with salt and pepper and blend until smooth. With the machine running, drizzle in the groundnut oil. Taste and adjust the seasoning, if necessary.

4 In a large bowl, combine the cos lettuce, Chinese leaf, red cabbage, radicchio, carrots, spring onion whites and jalapeño. Add the chicken, season with salt and pepper, add half the vinaigrette and toss. Add more vinaigrette, if necessary. Transfer to a platter and garnish with the chicken skin, nuts and spring onion greens. Arrange the lime quarters around the platter and serve.

1 head radicchio, halved, cored and thinly sliced

165g peeled carrot, grated

1 bunch spring onions, white and green parts separated, sliced 5mm thick

1 jalapeño chilli, finely chopped

140g salted roasted cashews

2 limes, each cut into 6 wedges

To Drink:

A Pinot Gris

Ming's tips:

If you're in a hurry, buy ready-roasted chicken from your supermarket or deli. If you can't get a large chicken, buy smaller birds to equal about 2.7kg.

At Blue Ginger we serve this salad with an extra garnish of fried wonton wrappers, which add great crunch. To make, cut the wrappers into 5mm-wide strips, fry them in rapeseed (canola) oil that's heated to 180°C, drain and salt. Add with the other garnishes.

Thai beef salad is an awesome blend of flavours and textures. There are many versions; mine combines the traditional rare grilled beef with a warm dressing made with chillies, fish sauce and lime juice, among other typical Thai ingredients. I westernise the dish, though, with the addition of carrots, cabbage and radicchio, whose soft crunch and slight bitterness are a terrific plus. I call for rump or stirloin steak to make this, but, really, you can use almost any cut. I've also had good luck with flank steak, which, besides being tasty, is easier on the pocket.

THAI BEEF SALAD

SERVES 4

6 tablespoons rapeseed (canola) oil

1 x 280–350g rump or
  sirloin steak, about 2.5cm thick

Sea salt and freshly ground
  black pepper

2 large shallots, finely chopped

1 bunch spring onions, white and
  green parts, thinly sliced,
  1 tablespoon of the greens
  reserved for garnish

3 bird's eye chillies, or 2 serrano
  chillies, with seeds, finely chopped

Juice of 3 limes

3 tablespoons fish sauce

1 small head white cabbage, cut into
  3mm-thick slices

1 large or 2 small heads radicchio,
  cut into 5mm-thick slices

2 large carrots, peeled and grated

1 Heat a medium sauté pan or cast-iron frying pan over a medium-high heat. Add 2 tablespoons of the oil and swirl to coat the pan. Season the steak with salt and pepper and cook, turning once, for 4–5 minutes per side until brown and medium-rare. Set aside and leave to rest for 10 minutes.

2 Return the pan to a medium heat. Add 1 tablespoon of the oil and swirl to coat the pan. When the oil is hot, add the shallots, spring onions and chillies, season with salt and pepper and sauté, stirring, for about 1 minute until soft. Remove from the heat, add the lime juice and fish sauce and whisk in the remaining 3 tablespoons rapeseed (canola) oil.

3 In a large bowl, combine the cabbage, radicchio and carrots, and toss with the warm vinaigrette. Adjust the seasoning, if necessary.

4 Slice the steak 5mm thick. Toss the steak and its juices with the salad, garnish with the reserved spring onions and serve.

Ming's tip:

Save any extra slaw to serve the next day. The recipe makes 5 slices of beef per person. If you want beef with your leftover slaw, cook 2 steaks instead.

Video tips:

Watch the video to learn how to achieve a perfectly cooked steak and prepare all the salad ingredients.

To Drink:
A chilled Gamay or a fruity wine

When travelling in Japan in the 90s, I fell in love with a vinaigrette commonly served there. It features ponzu – the acidic note – plus shallots and miso. I think of miso as soy sauce on steroids; it gives an umami punch to all sorts of dishes, as it does to this warm prawn salad. Included too are frisée and cherry tomatoes, great Western additions. You can cook the prawns in advance, refrigerate them and serve them in the salad cold, but I prefer them hot, as then they help wilt the frisée.

MISO-SHALLOT PRAWN FRISÉE SALAD

SERVES 4–6

2 large shallots, roughly chopped

2 heaped tablespoons shiro miso

1 tablespoon wasabi powder mixed with 2 tablespoons room-temperature water

2 tablespoons shoyu ponzu

120ml plus 1 tablespoon rapeseed (canola) oil

Freshly ground black pepper

1 teaspoon toasted sesame oil

450g medium raw prawns, peeled and deveined

Sea salt

115g peeled carrot, grated

2 frisée lettuces, cored, leaves torn, rinsed and dried

300g cherry tomatoes, halved

1 In a blender, combine the shallots, miso, wasabi and ponzu, and blend at high speed. With the machine running, add 1 tablespoon water then gradually drizzle in the 120ml rapeseed (canola) oil. Season with salt and pepper, blend in the sesame oil and 2 to 4 tablespoons water, and set aside.

2 Heat a medium sauté pan over a high heat. Add the remaining 1 tablespoon rapeseed (canola) oil and swirl to coat the pan. When the oil is hot, add the prawns, season with salt and pepper and sauté, stirring, for about 2 minutes until the prawns are cooked through.

3 In a large serving bowl, combine the carrots, frisée, tomatoes and prawns, and toss. Add enough vinaigrette to coat the salad lightly and toss. Taste to adjust the seasoning, toss and serve.

Ming's tip:

The recipe makes more vinaigrette than you'll need. Save the extra to make a chicken salad dressing that's lighter than the usual mayo-based kind.

To Drink:

A Pinot Grigio, like Alta Luna, from Italy, or a Pinot Blanc

People should use cranberries more often. They're tarter than any other fruit and make a superior vinegar replacement in vinaigrettes. I use them in just that way in this great barbecued chicken salad. The dressing, which also features grainy mustard and shallots, a classic French combo, pairs beautifully with the slight smokiness of the chicken. Served with crusty bread, this makes a great meal.

BARBECUED CHICKEN SALAD
with Cranberry–Mustard Vinaigrette

SERVES 4–6

60g sea salt, for brining,
    plus extra to season

65g granulated sugar

4 boneless, skinless chicken breasts

Freshly ground black pepper

2 tablespoons rapeseed (canola) oil, if
    grilling the chicken indoors

1 large or 2 small shallots, roughly
    chopped

2 tablespoons Pommerey mustard

100g cranberries

2 tablespoons naturally brewed
    soy sauce

240ml extra-virgin olive oil

3 frisée lettuces, cored, leaves torn,
    rinsed and dried

300g cherry tomatoes, halved

1 The day before, brine the chicken. In a large jug, combine the 60g salt and the sugar with 1.9 litres water and stir to dissolve the sugar and salt. Place the chicken in a bowl or saucepan large enough to hold it and the brine, and pour the brine over the chicken. If the chicken isn't covered, make more brine and add it to the bowl. Refrigerate overnight. Rinse the chicken and pat dry.

2 Preheat an outdoor barbecue to high and lightly oil the rack. Season the chicken with salt and pepper and cook, turning once for 4–5 minutes per side until just cooked through. Alternatively, heat a large griddle pan or cast-iron frying over a medium-high heat. Add the rapeseed (canola) oil and swirl to coat the pan. When the oil is hot, add the breast and sauté, turning once, for 4–5 minutes per side until cooked through, or until the tip of a paring knife inserted into the thickest part of the meat feels hot when removed. Transfer the chicken to a chopping board, leave to rest for 5 minutes, then slice lengthways into 5mm-thick strips.

3 Meanwhile, in a blender, combine the shallots, mustard, cranberries, soy sauce and 2 tablespoons water, and blend on a high speed until smooth. With the machine running, drizzle in the olive oil and season with salt and pepper.

4 In a large bowl, combine the chicken, frisée, tomatoes and half the vinaigrette. Season with salt and pepper, and add more vinaigrette until lightly coated. Transfer the salad to serving plates, drizzle with additional vinaigrette and serve.

To Drink:
A bright New World Sauvignon Blanc, like Isabel, from New Zealand

People who feel cheated when served a meatless main quickly embrace this salad. The flavours are vivid, and the crisp vegetables and succulent noodles contrast beautifully. A key to the dish's success is, interestingly, basil, which not only brightens the salad but ties all the flavours together. Another key is wok-cooking. Considering my ancestry, I'm partial to the technique, but none other produces the vibrancy that characterises this dish.

WOK-STIRRED VEGETABLES
and Rice Noodle Salad

SERVES 6

225g rice stick noodles
1 tablespoon rapeseed (canola) oil
1 tablespoon finely chopped garlic
1 tablespoon finely chopped fresh
   ginger
1 bunch spring onions, white and
   green parts separated, thinly sliced
½ white cabbage, halved, cored and
   cut into 1cm dice
Sea salt and freshly ground
   black pepper
2 medium red peppers, cut into
   1cm dice
225g peeled carrots, grated
4 tablespoons soy sauce
4 tablespoons rice vinegar
1 tablespoon sesame oil
20g basil leaves, cut
   into 5mm strips

1 Put the noodles in a large bowl and fill it with hot water to cover. When the noodles have softened, after about 15 minutes, drain, return to the bowl and set aside.

2 Heat a wok over a medium-high heat. Add the oil and swirl to coat the pan. When the oil is hot, add the garlic, ginger and spring onion whites and stir-fry for about 30 seconds until aromatic. Add the cabbage and stir-fry for about 1 minute until wilted. Season with salt and pepper, add the red pepper and carrots and toss. Add 2 tablespoons of the soy sauce and the vinegar, toss, remove from the heat and adjust the seasoning with salt and pepper, if necessary.

3 Add half the vegetables, the remaining 2 tablespoons soy sauce, the sesame oil and basil to the noodles. Mix well and season with salt and pepper.

4 Transfer the noodle mixture to a large serving platter, top with the remaining vegetables and garnish with the spring onion greens. Serve immediately.

Video tip:

Watch the video to learn my simple technique for peeling and chopping ginger and the easy way to slice basil.

To Drink:

A Pinot Blanc

No wonder that salmon is now such a popular fish. Besides being uniquely tasty, it has just the right fat content, and is delicious served hot, at room temperature or cold. For this salad, I've paired salmon with a bright-tasting vinaigrette, whose dominant orange flavour, both tangy and sweet, complements and beings out the sweetness of the fish. With some bread, this makes a delicious light meal, and is really perfect for summer.

SALMON SALAD
with Shallot–Orange Vinaigrette

SERVES 4

70g pine nuts

450g skinless salmon, preferably centre cut, cut into 2.5cm cubes

Sea salt and freshly ground black pepper

120ml plus 1 tablespoon extra-virgin olive oil

1 large shallot, thinly sliced

2 tablespoons Dijon mustard

1 tablespoon finely chopped fresh ginger

225g baby leaf and herb salad

4 oranges, juice and zest of 2, segments from 2

1 In a medium sauté pan, toast the pine nuts over a medium-low heat, stirring constantly, for 2–4 minutes until golden. Transfer to a small bowl and set aside.

2 Season the salmon with salt and pepper. Add 1 tablespoon of the oil to the pan, and swirl to coat it. Heat the oil and when hot, add the salmon and sauté, stirring occasionally, for 2–3 minutes until the salmon is medium-rare, or 4–5 minutes for cooked through. Transfer the salmon to a large bowl.

3 In the container of an immersion blender or in a standard blender, combine the shallot, mustard, ginger and orange juice. Season with salt and pepper and blend until the mixture is smooth. With the machine running, gradually drizzle in the 120ml oil to make an emulsion.

4 In a large salad bowl, add the baby leaf and herb salad, half the dressing and half the orange zest and segments. Season with salt and pepper and toss. The leaves should be lightly coated; add more dressing, if needed. Add the salmon and toss lightly. Garnish with the remaining zest and pine nuts and serve immediately.

Ming's tip:

To segment an orange easily, first cut off both ends deeply enough so that you can see the flesh. Using the knife, peel the orange just close enough to the flesh until no pith remains. Trim away any remaining pith, if necessary. Working over a bowl to catch the juice, cut between the membranes that separate the segments, releasing them. Squeeze the membranes to get any remaining juice to use as you wish.

To Drink:

An unoaked Chardonnay, like La Crema, from California

If you were ever a kid, you undoubtedly had your share of canned tomato soup. It's a classic, but the soup's even better homemade. Heart- and soul-warming, my version features quinoa, which not only tastes great but, because it's a complete protein, is good for you. Ginger adds zing, and carrots lend sweetness. This is the kind of satisfying, stick-to-the-ribs dish that cold weather was made for.

QUINOA AND TOMATO SOUP

SERVES 8

3 tablespoons extra-virgin olive oil

2 large onions, roughly chopped

1 tablespoon finely chopped fresh ginger

2 large carrots, peeled and cut into 5mm-thick rounds

4 celery sticks, thinly sliced

Sea salt and freshly ground black pepper

4 x 400g cans whole plum tomatoes

2 litres fresh chicken stock or low-sodium bought

60ml organic, wheat-free tamari

170g quinoa, rinsed

Parmesan cheese for garnish

1 Heat a large saucepan over a high heat. Add 2 tablespoons of the oil and swirl to coat the base. When the oil is hot, add the onions, ginger, carrots and celery, season with salt and pepper and sauté, stirring every few minutes, for 10–12 minutes until the vegetables are lightly caramelised.

2 Add the tomatoes with their juice. Break up the tomatoes and add the stock and tamari. Bring to a simmer and cook for about 10 minutes until the vegetables are soft.

3 Using an immersion blender, or a standard blender and working in batches, purée the soup. Add the quinoa, bring to a simmer and cook for about 12 minutes until the quinoa is just tender.

4 Transfer the soup to individual soup bowls, grate Parmesan over each and drizzle with the remaining tablespoon olive oil. Add a few grinds of pepper and serve.

Ming's tip:

This serves 8 amply; even so, you'll probably have leftover soup for another day.

To Drink:

Jasmine pearl or toasted rice green tea

I'm a soba noodle fanatic. In Japan, the noodles are often served as is with a dipping sauce of soy, dashi and spring onions. Why not, I wondered, use them in soup? Here's the result of my self-interrogation, a great soup, enhanced with sake, and served with a cool cucumber salad. This makes a great – and healthy – light lunch or first course.

SESAME SOBA NOODLE SOUP
with Cucumber Salad

SERVES 4

225–250g packet soba noodles

2 tablespoons rapeseed (canola) oil

2 large onions, thinly sliced

Sea salt and freshly ground
   black pepper

240ml sake

3 tablespoons naturally brewed
   soy sauce

1 teaspoon toasted sesame oil

2 litres fresh vegetable stock or
   low-sodium bought

1 heaped tablespoon wasabi powder
   mixed with 1 tablespoon room-
   temperature water

1 small cucumber, halved lengthways
   and very thinly sliced (see Tip)

1 tablespoon toasted sesame seeds

1 Fill a large bowl with water and add ice. In a large saucepan, cook the noodles in abundant salted water for about 7 minutes until al dente. Drain and transfer to the bowl of iced water. When the noodles are cold, drain well and set aside.

2 Return the pan to a medium-high heat. Add 1 tablespoon of the rapeseed (canola) oil and swirl to coat the base. When the oil is hot, add the onions, season with salt and pepper and sauté, stirring once, for 10–12 minutes until caramelised. Add the sake and cook, scraping the base of the pan to incorporate the brown bits, for about 30 seconds. Add 2 tablespoons of the soy sauce, the sesame oil and stock and bring to a simmer. Add the noodles and heat through.

3 Meanwhile, combine the wasabi, the remaining 1 tablespoon soy sauce and the remaining tablespoon rapeseed (canola) oil in a medium bowl. Add the cucumber, toss and season with salt and pepper. Add half the sesame seeds and toss again.

4 Divide the soup between 4 soup plates. Make a mound of the noodles in each, top with the cucumber salad, garnish with the remaining sesame seeds and serve.

Ming's tip:
If you have a mandolin, use it to slice the cucumbers.

Video tip:
Watch the video to learn my trick for cooling and draining the noodles.

To Drink:
Chilled TY KU Sake Black

My sweet potato craving goes back to childhood Thanksgivings, when they were served mashed and, yes, marshmallow-topped. My paternal grandfather, Yeh-Yeh, also loved the sweet potatoes, which, growing up, he bought hot from street vendors in China. This soup celebrates the sweet potato, boosted with garlic and ginger, its most complementary flavourings, I feel. This is everything you want from a soup – warming and good.

GARLIC–GINGER SWEET POTATO SOUP

SERVES 8

4 large sweet potatoes

1 tablespoon rapeseed (canola) oil

2 large onions, cut into 5mm-thick slices

2 tablespoons finely chopped garlic

2 tablespoons finely chopped fresh ginger

1 jalapeño chilli, with seeds, finely chopped

Sea salt and freshly ground black pepper

2 litres fresh chicken stock or low-sodium bought

2 tablespoons naturally brewed soy sauce

25g unsalted butter (optional)

2 tablespoons thinly sliced chives

1 Preheat the oven to 200°C/fan 180°C/Gas Mark 6. Wrap the sweet potatoes in foil, pierce them in several places with the point of a paring knife and bake for about 45 minutes until a fork pierces them easily. When cool enough to handle, scoop the sweet potato flesh into a bowl and set aside.

2 Heat a large heavy saucepan over a medium-high heat. Add the oil and swirl to coat the base. When the oil is hot, add the onions, garlic and ginger, season with salt and pepper and sauté, stirring, for 3–4 minutes until softened. Add the jalapeño and sauté, stirring, for 1 minute. Add the sweet potato, stock and soy sauce, taste to adjust the seasoning and bring to a simmer.

3 Using an immersion blender, purée the mixture. For a smoother texture, transfer the soup in batches to a standard blender or food processor and purée again. Alternatively, purée the mixture in batches in a blender only. With the machine running, add the butter, if using. Adjust the seasoning with salt and pepper. Divide the soup between serving bowls, garnish with the chives and serve.

To Drink:
A lager like Sam Adams

I first enjoyed pork stew in Santa Fe. It was made with Hatch green chillies, remarkable because their initial heat decrescendos to a lovely sweetness. They're difficult to find, though, and jalapeños work beautifully in the stew too. I include miso for the same reason I put it in other dishes – as a natural flavour enhancer. Added too are sweet potatoes and edamame for great textural contrast. Serve the stew with crusty wholemeal bread and you're in business.

CHILLI MISO PORK STEW

SERVES 6–8

4 jalapeño chillies
3 green peppers
1 tablespoon paprika
1 tablespoon chilli powder
1 tablespoon natural onion powder
1 tablespoon natural garlic powder
2 tablespoons sea salt, plus extra
   for seasoning
900g boneless pork shoulder,
   cut into 2.5cm cubes
3 tablespoons rapeseed (canola) oil,
   plus extra if needed
2 large onions, cut into 2.5cm pieces
1 tablespoon finely chopped garlic
Freshly ground black pepper
2 litres fresh chicken stock or
   low-sodium bought
4 tablespoons shiro miso
2 large sweet potatoes, peeled
   and cut into 1cm dice
300g shelled edamame
Crusty bread, for serving

To Drink:
A lager like Yanjing or an off-dry
Riesling like Leitz 'Eins Zwei Dry'

1 Turn a gas burner to high. Skewer the jalapeños on a metal skewer and place on the burner for 2–3 minutes until they bubble and turn black. When one side is charred, protecting your fingers with oven gloves, turn the skewer and char the jalapeños on the second side for 2–3 minutes. Alternatively, char the jalapeños under the grill. Transfer to a brown paper bag, close the bag and leave to steam for 5–10 minutes. This helps loosen the skin. Remove the jalapeños from the bag, and, with your fingers or damp kitchen paper, rub off the skin. Remove and discard the stem, seeds and veins. Repeat the procedure with the green peppers, turning them with tongs until they're blistered on all sides. Cut the peppers into 2.5cm pieces and transfer them and the chillies to a plate. Set aside.

2 In a medium bowl, combine the paprika and the chilli, onion and garlic powders. Add the 2 tablespoons salt and mix well. Add the pork, toss to coat it well and transfer to the fridge to flavour for at least 1 hour or overnight.

3 Heat a large heavy saucepan over a medium-high heat. Add 1 tablespoon of the oil and swirl to coat the base. Add half the pork and cook for 4–5 minutes until browned on all sides. Transfer the pork to a plate and set aside. Repeat with another tablespoon of oil and the remaining pork.

4 Wipe out the pan, heat over a medium-high heat and add the remaining 1 tablespoon oil. Swirl to coat the base, and when the oil is hot, add the onions and garlic and sauté, stirring, for 5–6 minutes until browned. Add the skinned chillies and peppers, and return the pork to the pan. Add the stock and bring to a simmer. Place the miso in a sieve, dip it into the stock and whisk to dissolve the miso into the soup. Adjust the seasoning with salt and pepper and simmer for about 1½ hours until the pork is tender.

5 Add the sweet potatoes and edamame and simmer for 15–20 minutes until the sweet potatoes are tender. Transfer to individual bowls and serve with the bread.

Ming's tip:

You can make this dish in a pressure cooker to save time. Follow the instructions up to the final simmering and lock the lid in place according to the manufacturer's instructions. When the steam begins to hiss out of the cooker, reduce the heat to low, just enough to maintain a very weak whistle, and cook for 30 minutes. Release the pressure, add the potatoes and edamames, lock on the lid and cook for a further 15 minutes.

Everyone loves chilli. This super version contains turkey, pork and lamb mince, plus black beans. It's also easy to cook and satisfies everybody, kids included. I usually hand round cornbread with this, but sometimes I'm tempted to serve it as the Skyline Diner in Dayton, Ohio, served its chilli when I was growing up – on pasta. Why not?

BEST 3-MEAT CHILLI

SERVES 6–8

2 tablespoons rapeseed (canola) oil

2 large onions, cut into 1cm dice

2 tablespoons thinly sliced garlic

3 jalapeño chillies, 2 finely chopped, and 1 cut into thin rings for garnish

Sea salt and freshly ground black pepper

2 tablespoons paprika

2 tablespoons chilli powder

2 tablespoons ground ginger

450g minced turkey

450g pork mince

450g lamb mince

2 x 400g can tomatoes, diced

1 x 400g can black beans, drained

150g shelled edamame

4 tablespoons naturally brewed soy sauce

1 litre fresh chicken stock or low-sodium bought, or as needed

175-350g cooked 50-50 White and Brown Rice (page 13)

250g natural Greek yogurt

Large handful chopped fresh coriander

1 Heat a large flameproof casserole dish over a medium-high heat. Add the oil and swirl to coat the base. When the oil is hot, add the onions, garlic and finely chopped jalapeños. Season with salt and pepper and sauté, stirring, for about 6 minutes until the onions are lightly coloured.

2 Add the paprika, chilli powder and ground ginger. Season with salt and pepper and sauté, stirring, for 30 seconds. Add the 3 meat minces, season with salt and pepper and sauté, breaking them up, for about 2 minutes. Add the tomatoes with their juice and stir, scraping the base of the pan to incorporate any browned bits. Add the black beans, edamame, soy sauce and enough stock to cover the meat. Add the rice, if using, and simmer for about 30 minutes until the chilli is reduced by one-quarter, or 1 hour if not using rice. Adjust the seasoning with salt and pepper.

3 Transfer the chilli to individual serving bowls. Garnish with the yogurt, coriander and jalapeño rings and serve.

Ming's tip:

This dish makes enough chilli to store and serve on another day.

To Drink:

A beer

This 'Nawleens' speciality has many versions. My favourite ones, though, include 'surf and turf', seafood and meat like ham or sausages. This version features prawn and Chinese sausages or bacon, but in place of the usual flour- and oil-based roux thickening, I use a cornflour mixture, which makes a lighter dish that's also gluten-free. Another bow to the East, besides the sausage, is the sambal, which gives the gumbo real kick. There's okra in it too, which couldn't be more traditional. Served with cornbread, as I like to do, this is a terrific full-meal dish that's particularly great for company.

SAMBAL PRAWN GUMBO

SERVES 6–8

1 tablespoon rapeseed (canola) oil

4 Chinese sausages, sliced 5mm thick; or 4 rashers bacon, cut 5mm thick

1 tablespoon finely chopped garlic

2 large onions, finely chopped

Sea salt and freshly ground black pepper

1 head celery, sticks cut into 5mm-thick slices

2 large peppers, red and green, finely chopped

1 tablespoon paprika

2 tablespoons sambal or hot sauce

4 tablespoons organic Worcestershire sauce

450g okra, stems removed, cut into 1cm-thick slices

2 litres fresh chicken stock or low-sodium bought

2 tablespoons cornflour mixed with 2 tablespoons water

900g medium raw prawns, peeled and deveined

1–1.3kg cooked 50-50 White and Brown Rice (page 13), for serving

To Drink:

A Pinot Gris like Trimbach Reserve Personnelle

1 Heat a large flameproof casserole over a medium-high heat. Add the oil and swirl to coat the base. When the oil is hot, add the sausages and cook for 1–2 minutes until their fat is rendered. If using bacon, cook it for 3–4 minutes until crisp.

2 Add the garlic and onions, season with salt and black pepper and sauté, stirring, for about 2 minutes until translucent. Add the celery, peppers and paprika, adjust the seasoning with salt and pepper and sauté, stirring, for 2–3 minutes until tender. Add the sambal and Worcestershire sauce, and sauté, stirring, for 1 minute. Add the okra, stir and season with salt. Add the stock, adjust the seasoning, bring to a simmer and cook, covered, for about 10 minutes until the mixture is reduced by a fifth.

3 Whisk in the cornflour mixture, then add the prawns, return to a simmer and cook for about 2 minutes until cooked through. Adjust the seasoning with salt and pepper.

4 Divide the rice between soup plates. Top with the gumbo and serve.

Video tip:

Watch the video to learn all about okra.

CHAPTER 3

Seafood

Seafood invites invention. It's a great canvas for many flavouring approaches. Glazes and marinades, to name two, flavour seafood deliciously with little work for the cook.

Take Soy-Sake Salmon with Almond Fried Rice, an update of trout almondine that's powered by the fish's preliminary bath in soy sauce, sake, honey and lime juice. Ginger–Citrus Swordfish with Fennel Salad benefits similarly from an orange–lemon marinade, which is also cooked and used to dress the accompanying salad. Grilled Miso-Glazed Salmon with Lime–Cucumber Orzo is glazed with a miso mixture that yields a complementary sweetness and irresistibly crisp, caramelised skin.

Succulent, quick-cooking prawns are very flavour-friendly. Spicy Prawns with Mango and Rice Noodles contrast sambal heat, mango sweetness and chewy noodles for truly exciting eating. Tempura Prawns with Avocado and Ponzu Dipping Sauce not only delivers the best tempura prawns ever but accompanies it with buttery-crisp tempura avocado.

Seafood is also great for entertaining. Thai Seafood Noodle Pot, a meal in one featuring clams, mussels and rice vermicelli, is an elbows-on-the-table treat, while Banana Leaf-Wrapped Chilli Halibut – the fish is cooked in parcels that are opened at table – makes any dinner party deluxe. Buy the most pristine seafood you can get, flavour it imaginatively, cook it to perfection – I show you how – and seafood makes the party.

I had my first trout almondine in the only French restaurant in Dayton, Ohio, my home town. I loved the contrast of the crunchy almonds and buttery fish. I honour that classic combo of fish and almonds in this recipe, but use salmon, a richer, more luscious fish, instead of trout. The salmon gets a piquant sweet–sour marinade that's also used to make a pan sauce. The almonds go into the rice, which also includes spring onions and scrambled eggs. This is a homey dish that's also great for casual entertaining.

SOY–SAKE SALMON
with Almond Fried Rice

SERVES 4

4 x 175g skinless centre-cut salmon fillets
120ml plus 1 tablespoon naturally brewed soy sauce
120ml sake
2 tablespoons runny honey
Juice from 2 limes
110g flaked almonds
3 large eggs
Sea salt and freshly ground black pepper
6 tablespoons rapeseed (canola) oil
1 tablespoon finely chopped fresh ginger
2 bunches spring onions, white and green parts, sliced 5mm thick, 1 tablespoon of the greens reserved
1kg cooked jasmine or basmati rice or other long-grain rice (see Tip, page 13)
25g unsalted butter

To Drink:

A chilled Sake, like TY KU Black, or a crisp Chardonnay, like Éric Chevalier, from France

1 Put the salmon in a deep plate. In a small bowl, combine the 120ml soy sauce, sake, honey and lime juice. Pour over the salmon and marinate for at least 15 minutes and up to 1 hour.

2 In a wok, toast the almonds over a medium heat, stirring constantly, for 3–5 minutes until golden. Transfer to a small bowl and set aside.

3 Line a large plate with kitchen paper. In a small bowl, beat the eggs and season with salt and pepper.

4 Heat the wok over a high heat. Add 4 tablespoons of the oil and swirl to coat the pan. When the oil is almost smoking, add the eggs, which will puff. Stir-fry for about 10 seconds until scrambled, then transfer to the kitchen paper to drain.

5 Reduce the heat to medium-high. Add 1 tablespoon of the oil to the pan and swirl to coat the pan. Add the ginger and spring onions and sauté, stirring, for about 30 seconds. Season with salt and pepper, add the rice, almonds, eggs and remaining 1 tablespoon soy sauce and stir to blend, breaking up the eggs. Adjust the seasoning, if necessary, and transfer to a large bowl.

6 Remove the salmon from the marinade and pat dry. Reserve the marinade.

7 Heat a large sauté pan over a medium-high heat. Add the remaining tablespoon oil and swirl to coat the base. When the oil is hot, add the salmon nicest side down and cook for about 1 minute until golden. Flip the salmon, lower the heat to medium-low and cook for 2 minutes. Increase the heat to medium, turn the salmon on one edge and cook for a further 2 minutes. Turn onto the remaining edge and cook for another 2 minutes until medium cooked. Transfer to a plate.

8 Wipe out the pan. Add the marinade and bring to a simmer over a medium heat. Add the reserved spring onions. Cook for 1–2 minutes to reduce the marinade by half. Remove from the heat and whisk in the butter. Adjust the seasoning.

9 Divide the rice between individual plates and top with the salmon. Drizzle the fish with the pan sauce and serve.

Ming's tip:

If you get tail-end fillets, sauté them on 2 sides only, not on their edges.

I'm so happy that swordfish is available again after a decade of being overfished. The key to making the best of this wonderful fish is to marinate it first in a tenderising bath that contains an acid – here, orange and lemon juices. Nothing goes better with citrus than soy sauce, and that's in the marinade too. Fennel, a vegetable I love, accompanies the fish – it's also a sucker for citrus, so the whole dish is deliciously harmonious. This is an all-season main course – light enough for summer, but also great in winter when citrus fruit is at its best.

GINGER–CITRUS SWORDFISH
with Fennel Salad

SERVES 4

2 large fennel bulbs, halved, cored and shaved (see Tip), fronds reserved for garnish

4 large oranges, juice of 2, the others segmented, 7 segments reserved for garnish

Juice of 1 lemon

1 tablespoon naturally brewed soy sauce

1 tablespoon finely chopped fresh ginger

675g skinless swordfish steak, preferably centre cut, bloodline removed, cut into eight 2.5cm x 2.5cm logs

Sea salt and freshly ground black pepper

2 tablespoons fennel seeds, crushed

4 tablespoons extra-virgin olive oil

1 Put the shaved fennel in a large bowl. Set aside.

2 In a medium bowl, combine the orange and lemon juices, soy sauce and ginger until blended. Add the swordfish, turn gently to coat and marinate for 10 minutes.

3 Transfer the fish to a large plate and pat dry. Season with salt and pepper and sprinkle evenly with the fennel seeds. Reserve the marinade.

4 Heat a large sauté pan over a medium heat. Add 1 tablespoon of the oil and swirl to coat the pan. When the oil is hot, add the fish and sauté on all sides for 1–2 minutes per side until it is almost cooked through. Transfer the fish to a plate.

5 Put the marinade in a small saucepan and bring to a simmer over a medium-high heat. Whisk in the remaining 3 tablespoons oil and season with salt and pepper. Add all but the reserved orange segments to the bowl with the fennel. Add 4 tablespoons of the marinade, toss and season with salt and pepper.

6 Divide the fennel salad between serving plates. Top with the swordfish and drizzle with the remaining marinade. Garnish with the fennel fronds and orange segments and serve.

To Drink:

A bright New World Sauvignon Blanc, like Dog Point Vineyard, from New Zealand

Ming's tip:

A mandoline makes shaving the fennel a breeze. Kyocera makes an inexpensive one that works like a charm.

Video tip:

Watch the video to learn how to select the freshest swordfish and correctly prepare it.

The combination of hot and sweet is famously exciting and gets full play here with sambal-spiced prawns and luscious mango. The mango brings out the prawns' sweetness and vice versa. Rice noodles, like tofu, are remarkable flavour-carriers, and thus ensure a super-tasty dish; they're also delightfully chewy. This is great for a simple weeknight supper, but you'll enjoy it as a weekend lunch too.

SPICY PRAWNS WITH MANGO
and Rice Noodles

SERVES 4

450g mangetout
Sea salt
1 packet (about 250g) rice sticks
3 tablespoons rapeseed (canola) oil
1 tablespoon finely chopped fresh
  ginger
1 bunch spring onions, white and
  green parts, thinly sliced,
  1 tablespoon of the greens
  reserved for garnish
Freshly ground black pepper
450g medium raw prawns, peeled
  and deveined
1 tablespoon sambal or other
  hot sauce
2 mangoes, peeled, stoned and cut
  into 1cm pieces
240ml fresh chicken stock or
  low-sodium bought
1 tablespoon rice vinegar or
  lemon juice

1 Fill a large bowl with water and add ice cubes. Blanch the mangetout in abundant salted water for about 45 seconds until bright green. Drain the mangetout and transfer to the iced water. Transfer the cooking water to a large bowl. When the mangetout are cold, drain them and pat dry. Set aside.

2 Add the noodles to the bowl with the cooking water. (If the noodles aren't submerged, add hot water.) When the noodles have softened, after about 15 minutes, drain and set aside.

3 Heat a wok or large sauté pan over a medium-high heat. Add 2 tablespoons of the oil and swirl to coat the pan. When the oil is hot, add the ginger and all but the reserved spring onions. Season with salt and pepper and sauté, stirring, for 30 seconds–1 minute until aromatic. Add the prawns and sauté, stirring, for about 2 minutes until the prawns are almost cooked through. Season with salt and pepper, add the sambal and mangoes and sauté for about 1 minute until the prawns are cooked through. Add the mangetout, noodles and stock and simmer, tossing, for 3–4 minutes until the liquid is reduced by three-quarters. Add the vinegar and season with salt and pepper. Transfer to a platter, garnish with the reserved spring onion greens and serve.

To Drink:
A Riesling, like Hugel, from Alsace

Steaming noodle pots – meal-in-one dishes that contain noodles and other fresh ingredients – are a Southeast Asian staple. My Thai-influenced version features mussels and clams plus rice vermicelli for great texture. Shellfish retain all their flavour when cooked in stock, as here, and the taste-combo of chilli heat, fish sauce, lime juice and shallots is winning, to say the least. This is quickly done and couldn't be more welcome for cold-weather dining.

THAI SEAFOOD NOODLE POT

SERVES 4

40g polenta (cornmeal)

450g fresh British carpetshell (palourde) clams or New Zealand Littleneck clams

1 packet (about 250g) rice vermicelli

1 tablespoon rapeseed (canola) oil

3 large shallots, thinly sliced

2 bird's eye chillies or 1 jalapeño chilli, thinly sliced

Six 7.5cm x 5mm-thick slices fresh ginger

Sea salt and freshly ground black pepper

450g fresh mussels, scrubbed and debearded

240ml white wine

1.4 litres fresh chicken stock or low-sodium bought, or vegetable stock

2 tablespoons fish sauce

Juice of 2 limes

450g medium raw prawns, peeled and deveined

Leaves from ½ bunch Thai or ordinary basil, plus extra for garnish

1 Fill a large bowl with water. Add the polenta, stir and add the clams. Leave the clams to purge for at least 1 hour and up to 3. Rinse, drain the clams well and set aside. Discard the water and polenta.

2 Put the noodles in a large bowl and fill it with hot water to cover. When the noodles have softened, after about 15 minutes, drain and set aside.

3 Heat a large saucepan or wok over a high heat. Add the oil and swirl to coat the base. When the oil is hot, add the shallots, chillies and ginger and sauté, stirring, for about 30 seconds until fragrant. Season with salt and pepper. Add the clams, toss and cook for about 4 minutes until the clams start to open. Add the mussels and wine, toss and cook for about 1 minute until the wine is reduced by half. Add the stock, stir in the fish sauce and add half of the lime juice. Adjust the seasoning with salt and pepper, cover, and cook for 5–6 minutes until the shellfish have opened, or less if the clams are small. Add the noodles, prawns and basil and bring to a simmer. Cover and cook for 2–3 minutes until the prawns are cooked through, then remove from the heat, adjust the seasoning with salt and pepper and add the remaining lime juice. (Discard any unopened shellfish.) Transfer to a large serving bowl, garnish with the basil and serve.

Video tip:

Watch the video to learn about preparing clams and mussels.

To Drink:

An off-dry Chenin Blanc like Remy Pannier Vouvray

Is there anything better than crisp tempura prawns? My version is particularly delicate, thanks to a batter made from rice flour, soda water and beer, which adds a pleasingly yeasty taste and ups the crispness ante. If you've never had tempura avocado, you haven't lived. Its rich, buttery flesh is a perfect foil for its crisp exterior. Add ponzu dipping sauce and you're in for seriously great eating.

TEMPURA PRAWNS WITH AVOCADO
and Ponzu Dipping Sauce

SERVES 4–6

310g rice flour

1 teaspoon togarashi or cayenne,
   or to taste

160ml soda water, or more if needed

120ml beer, or more if needed

1 bunch spring onions, white and
   green parts separated, thinly sliced

Rapeseed (canola) oil for frying

12 raw king prawns, peeled,
   deveined and butterflied (see Tip)

Sea salt

2 ripe-firm avocados, halved, each
   half cut into 3 wedges

240ml ponzu

1 tablespoon finely chopped fresh
   ginger

1 Put the rice flour and togarashi in a large bowl and whisk in the soda water and beer gradually until the mixture has the consistency of pancake batter. Stir in the spring onion whites and half the greens. Set aside.

2 Line a large plate with kitchen paper. Fill a deep heavy saucepan one-third full with oil and heat over a medium-high heat. When the oil is 180°C, and working in batches of 4 or 5, dip the prawns into the batter, shake off any excess and add to the oil. Fry the prawns for 2–3 minutes until golden. With a slotted spoon, transfer the prawns to the kitchen paper to drain. Season with salt and transfer the fried prawns to a serving platter.

3 Return the oil to 180°C. Dip the avocado into the batter, drain and fry for 2–3 minutes until golden. Transfer to the kitchen paper to drain. Salt.

4 Meanwhile, in a medium serving bowl, combine the ponzu, ginger and the remaining spring onion greens. Arrange the prawns on a platter, surround with the avocado and serve immediately with the dipping sauce on the side.

Ming's tips:

To butterfly the prawns, after deveining, place the prawns on a flat surface and slice carefully across the open side towards but not through the side opposite. Unfold the prawn, pressing it gently against your work surface.

If you don't have a frying thermometer, you can tell when the oil is hot enough for frying by dribbling a bit of batter from the end of a chopstick into it. If the batter puffs up and floats, the oil is ready.

You can fry the prawns and the avocado together, in batches, rather than cooking them individually.

To Drink:

A sparkling rosé like Je T'aime Brut Rose or beer like Yanjing

I love this dish of crisp caramelised salmon paired with sprightly lime-flavoured orzo. Miso, the basis of the glaze, has to be one of my favourite ingredients – it's packed with flavour. But its natural saltiness needs to be toned down, and that's just what sake, also used in the glaze, does here. The light and freshly acidic orzo balances the richness of the fish for a marriage made in – well, you know.

GRILLED MISO-GLAZED SALMON
with Lime – Cucumber Orzo

SERVES 4

80ml shiro miso
3 tablespoons runny honey
180ml sake
80ml rapeseed (canola) oil, plus 1
 tablespoon if needed
4 x 175–200g salmon fillets,
 preferably centre cut, skin on
Sea salt
290g orzo, preferably
 wholemeal
2 tablespoons extra-virgin olive oil
1 large cucumber, diced
1 bunch spring onions, white and
 green parts, sliced 5mm thick
Juice of 2 limes
Freshly ground black pepper

1 In a blender, combine the miso, honey and sake and blend. With the machine running, drizzle in the 80ml rapeseed (canola) oil and blend until the mixture is emulsified. Put the salmon in a small non-reactive bowl and pour the marinade over it, spooning the marinade under and around the fillets to make sure they're evenly coated. Cover with cling film and refrigerate for 12–24 hours, turning once or twice.

2 Place the grill or oven shelf in the middle position and preheat the grill or oven on the grill setting. Fill a large bowl with water and add ice cubes. In a large saucepan, cook the pasta in abundant salted water for about 7 minutes until al dente; drain and add to the iced water. When the pasta is cold, drain the pasta. Return the pasta to the bowl, and toss with 1 tablespoon of the olive oil. Add the cucumber, spring onions, lime juice and remaining 1 tablespoon olive oil. Season with salt and pepper, toss and set aside.

3 Remove the salmon from the marinade and place it on kitchen paper to drain. Season the skin side with pepper. Preheat a large ovenproof sauté pan under the preheated grill or in the oven for about 10 minutes until very hot. Remove and spray with non-stick cooking spray or brush with 1 tablespoon rapeseed (canola) oil. Add the salmon skin side up, transfer to the grill or oven and grill for 7 minutes for medium or 10 minutes for well done. For very crisp skin, transfer the salmon to the top shelf and grill, watching carefully to avoid burning, for 15–30 seconds. Transfer the orzo to a platter or divide between 4 individual plates. Top with the salmon, skin side up, and serve.

To Drink:

A Chardonnay, like A to Z, from
Oregon or TY KU Sake Black

The best food I've enjoyed in Singapore is sold in seafood stalls. Their chilli-fired skate in banana leaves is dynamite in more ways than one. Here's my version, which replaces the skate with delicious halibut. The fish is chilli-seasoned, wrapped in the leaves – or in paper and foil, if you wish – and baked. The parcels are opened at the table, where they release super-fragrant steam. Talk about aromatherapy!

BANANA LEAF-WRAPPED CHILLI HALIBUT

SERVES 4

2 tablespoons rapeseed (canola) oil

2 red jalapeño chillies, finely chopped

1 tablespoon finely chopped fresh ginger

2 red onions, diced

1 teaspoon paprika

2 tablespoons fish sauce

2 limes, 1 juiced, the other cut into 4 wedges

Sea salt and freshly ground black pepper

4 banana leaves

4 x 175g halibut fillets, preferably centre cut

To Drink:
A Gewürztraminer

Ming's tip:
I call for red jalapeños, which are slightly hotter than the green, but you can certainly use the ordinary kind.

1 Preheat the oven to 200°C/fan 180°C/Gas Mark 6.

2 Heat a large ovenproof sauté pan over a medium-high heat. Add 1 tablespoon of the oil and swirl to coat the pan. When the oil is hot, add the jalapeños, ginger and onions and sauté, stirring, for about 4 minutes until the onions are soft. Add the paprika, stir and add the fish sauce. Remove the pan from the heat and add the lime juice. Toss, season with salt and pepper and transfer to a medium bowl. If using banana leaves, wipe out the sauté pan and set aside.

3 Place a banana leaf on your work surface with a wide side near you. Alternatively, cut 4 sheets each of baking paper and foil about 30cm square and place a banana leaf or sheet of paper on your work surface. Smear one-eighth of the chilli mixture on the centre of the leaf or sheet and place one of the halibut pieces, nicest side up, in the centre of the leaf or paper with the widest side parallel to the wide side of the wrapper. Season with salt and pepper and smear with another eighth of the chilli mixture. Bring the near side of the wrapper over the fish, then fold the far side over the first. Turn in the sides to enclose the fish completely. If using a banana leaf, secure the parcel with butcher's twine; if using paper, wrap the parcel in the foil and close to seal. Repeat with the remaining chilli mixture and pieces of fish.

4 If using banana leaves, heat the sauté pan over a medium heat. Add the remaining 1 tablespoon oil and swirl to coat the pan. When the oil is hot, add the fish, nicer side down, and sauté for about 1 minute until the leaf browns slightly. If using paper and foil, skip this step and transfer the parcels to the pan. Transfer to the oven and bake for 8–10 minutes until the fish is just cooked through. Test by inserting the tip of a paring knife into the fish for 3 seconds; if it emerges hot, the fish is done. Alternatively, a thermometer inserted into the fish will read 55°C.

5 Cut the twine from the parcels or remove the foil. Transfer the parcels to plates, folded side down if wrapped in banana leaves, and open them at the table with sharp scissors. Serve with the lime wedges on the side.

Having lived in New England for more than 20 years, I've had my share of cod. It's an unassuming fish, but one with great texture and subtle flavour. Here, the fish is coated in spring onion-flavoured panko, fried until golden and served on red onions and chard. Swiss chard is an underused vegetable – I think of it as a cross between spinach and kale – that when properly cooked, as here, brings raves.

SPRING ONION – PANKO COD
with Red Onions and Swiss Chard

SERVES 4

125g all-purpose flour

3 large eggs

120g panko breadcrumbs

1 heaped teaspoon ground white pepper

1 heaped teaspoon natural garlic powder

2 bunches spring onions, white and green parts separated, thinly sliced

4 x 175g cod fillets

Sea salt and freshly ground black pepper

4 tablespoons extra-virgin olive oil

2 red onions, thinly sliced

1 tablespoon finely chopped fresh ginger

1 bunch Swiss chard, bottom stems cut away, leaves cut into 5mm ribbons

Juice and zest of 1 lemon, plus lemon slices for garnish

1 Preheat the oven to 180°C/fan 160°C/Gas Mark 4. Put the flour, eggs and panko in separate shallow dishes. Add the white pepper and garlic powder to the flour and blend. Beat the eggs with 2 tablespoons water until well combined. Add all but 3 tablespoons of the spring onion greens to the panko and stir to mix.

2 Dry the cod with kitchen paper and season with salt and pepper. Dredge the cod in the flour, dip in the egg and drain the excess, then dredge in the panko mixture. Transfer to a large plate.

3 Heat a large ovenproof sauté pan over a medium-high heat. Add 2 tablespoons of the oil and swirl to coat the pan. When the oil is hot, add the fish and sauté, turning once, for about 1 minute per side until golden. Transfer to a large plate and set aside.

4 Wipe out the pan, add 1 tablespoon oil and swirl to coat the pan. When the oil is hot, add the spring onion whites, onions and ginger and sauté, stirring, for about 2 minutes until the onions are soft. Add the chard stems and sauté for 30 seconds, stirring, then add the leaves. Season with salt and pepper, add the lemon juice and zest and sauté, stirring, for about 1 minute until the chard has started to soften. Top with the fish, transfer to the oven and bake for 10–12 minutes until the fish is just cooked through, with an internal temperature of 55°C. Transfer the chard to serving plates and top with the cod. Drizzle with the remaining 1 tablespoon oil, garnish with the spring onion greens and serve with the lemon slices on the side.

To Drink:
An unoaked Chardonnay like Louis Latour Saint-Veran

Poaching salmon in olive oil – simmering it, actually, in an oil-based tapenade – ensures fish that's lusciously tender. You'll want to try this technique with other fish, like tuna or halibut. Flavoured with Thai basil, the tapenade is not only used as cooking medium but is served over the fish. I like to accompany this with couscous, but you could also serve it with crusty bread.

OLIVE OIL-POACHED SALMON
with Tomato Tapenade

SERVES 4

240ml extra-virgin olive oil

1 tablespoon fermented black beans

175g pitted Niçoise olives or other oil-cured black olives

1 large onion, thinly sliced

2 x 400g cans plum tomatoes, drained, crushed by hand to remove as much juice as possible and roughly chopped

Sea salt and freshly ground black pepper

4 x 175–225g skinless salmon fillets, any pin bones removed, cut into fingers approximately 13cm x 2.5cm x 2.5cm

Leaves from 1 bunch Thai basil or ordinary basil

60g wild rocket

3 lemons, juice of 1, zest of another, the third cut into wedges

1 Preheat the oven to 200°C/fan 180°C/Gas Mark 6. Put the oil in a flameproof, 23cm-square straight-sided baking dish, preferably with a lid. Add the black beans, olives and onion and heat over a medium heat until the mixture simmers. Continue to simmer for about 3 minutes until the onion has begun to soften. Add the tomatoes, season with salt and pepper and simmer for about 8 minutes until the tomatoes have melted.

2 Transfer three-quarters of the tapenade to a medium bowl. Season the salmon with salt and pepper. Add the salmon to the pan and top with a handful of the basil. Spoon the remaining tapenade over it so that the fish is completely submerged. Cover with the lid or foil and bake the salmon for 7–9 minutes for medium. Place a handful of the rocket on individual plates, drizzle with the lemon juice and season with salt and pepper. Using a slotted spoon, transfer the salmon to the plates atop the rocket, spoon over the tapenade, garnish with the lemon zest and serve.

Video tip:

Watch the video to learn all about umami.

To Drink:

A Blanc de Blanc Champagne like Charles de Fere Brut Reserve or Gosset Brut Excellence

CHAPTER 4

Meat

When asked if I like meat, I raise my hand. High. There's nothing quite as satisfying as a juicy steak, a sweet pork roast or a good, slow-cooked shank. But they're just the start. The recipes here take anyone's meat craving for a major ride.

Case in point: Teriyaki Skirt Steak with Garlic Potato Mash, a great family dish that transforms the time-tested marinated steak dish by adding potatoes and a ginger–citrus drizzle. Peppers Stuffed with Spicy Pork Fried Rice get their wallop from a stuffing that includes, besides pork, a fried rice mixture flavoured with ginger and garlic. And Pork Chops with Dried Cranberry–Apple Sweet Potato Hash amps up the humble pork chop and sweet potato pairing by adding a tempting foil of dried fruit and tart apples.

Retooling traditional dishes is my pleasure, but that doesn't mean the 'new' dish has to be fancy. Caramelised Onion and Beef 'Loco-Moco', based on the traditional Hawaiian rib-sticker of beef burger patties and fried eggs, gets a simplified, family-pleasing take. Braised 8-Spice Lamb Shoulder with Couscous is another homey dish that friends adore too. For family or company, serve meat and its fans rejoice.

When my kids smell this dish cooking – the aroma of garlic, ginger, caramelised sugar and seared steak combined – there's no question that plates will be cleaned. Adults are equally enthusiastic, so this is a family dish par excellence. Garlic lovers particularly rejoice when they taste the mashers, which are made with roasted garlic heads. Need I say more?

TERIYAKI SKIRT STEAK
with Garlic Potato Mash

SERVES 4

MARINADE
240ml naturally brewed soy sauce
1 tablespoon finely chopped garlic
1 tablespoon finely chopped fresh
 ginger
1 bunch spring onions, green and
 white parts separated, thinly sliced
2 tablespoons light or dark brown
 sugar
Juice and zest of 2 oranges,
 1 tablespoon zest reserved
 for garnish

900g skirt steak, trimmed
 and cut into 4 equal pieces
6 Yukon Gold or Estima potatoes,
 washed
2 large or 4 small heads garlic
Sea salt and freshly ground
 black pepper
1 tablespoon rapeseed (canola) oil
15g unsalted butter
370g fat-free natural Greek yogurt

To Drink:

A Meritage

1 For the marinade, in a large bowl, combine the soy sauce, finely chopped garlic, ginger, spring onion whites, sugar, orange juice and all but the reserved zest and stir. Add the steak, turn to coat and marinate for at least 6 and up to 12 hours, refrigerated. Remove the meat and transfer the marinade to a small saucepan.

2 Preheat the oven to 180°C/fan 160°C/Gas Mark 4. Wrap the potatoes in foil and pierce several times with a fork. Cut the tops off the garlic heads, season with salt and pepper, wrap individually in foil and place in a small baking dish. Transfer the potatoes and garlic to the oven. Bake for 45 minutes–1 hour until soft and tender. Transfer the potatoes to a medium bowl and the garlic to a plate and set aside.

3 Heat a large cast-iron frying pan or ovenproof frying pan over a high heat. Add the oil and swirl to coat the pan. Remove the steak from the marinade and season with salt and pepper on both sides. When the oil is hot, add the steak and sauté for 2–3 minutes per side until it colours. Transfer the steak in the pan to the oven and roast for 8–10 minutes for medium-rare (55°C on a meat thermometer inserted into the thickest part of the steak) or 10–12 minutes for medium (60°C). Transfer the steak to a chopping board, leave to rest for 10 minutes and then cut into 5mm-thick slices.

4 Meanwhile, bring the marinade to the boil over a medium heat. Lower the heat and simmer for about 6 minutes until the marinade is reduced by one-quarter. Remove from the heat and whisk in the butter.

5 Squeeze the garlic from the cloves into the bowl with the potatoes and, with a potato masher or 2 large forks, mash everything roughly, skin and all. Add the yogurt and season with salt and pepper. Stir to blend.

6 Divide the potatoes between 4 individual plates. Top with the steak, drizzle with the sauce, garnish with the reserved zest and the spring onion greens and serve.

I love Hawaiian food – from big-eye tuna to loco-moco, a seriously rib-sticking breakfast dish of rice topped with beef burger patties, onions and fried eggs. Here's my simpler, more refined version that works beautifully for lunch or a homey supper. Kids dig right in, and so do adults. You can of course have loco-moco for breakfast – in which case I advise major post-meal surfing.

CARAMELISED ONION AND BEEF
'Loco-Moco'

SERVES 4

3 tablespoons rapeseed (canola) oil
3 large onions, sliced 5mm thick
Sea salt and freshly ground
   black pepper
675g beef mince
2 bunches spring onions, white and
   green parts, sliced 5mm thick,
   1 tablespoon greens reserved
   for garnish
1 tablespoon finely chopped garlic
1 tablespoon plus 1 teaspoon
   naturally brewed soy sauce
480ml fresh beef or chicken stock or
   low-sodium bought
1 tablespoon cornflour mixed with
   1 tablespoon water
4 large eggs
1kg cooked 50-50 White and Brown
   Rice (page 13)

1 Heat a large heavy sauté pan or wok over a medium-high heat. Add 1 tablespoon oil and swirl to coat the pan. When the oil is hot, add the onions, season with salt and pepper and cook on one side for 8–10 minutes until caramelised. Turn, cook on the second side for about 5 minutes, then set the onions aside. Reserve the pan.

2 Meanwhile, in a medium bowl, combine the beef mince, all but the reserved spring onions, the garlic and 1 tablespoon of the soy sauce and season with pepper. Mix and form gently into 4 patties about 1cm thick.

3 Heat the pan over a medium-high heat, add 1 tablespoon of the oil and swirl to coat the pan. Season the patties on both sides with salt and pepper, transfer to the pan and cook, turning once, for about 4 minutes for medium-rare or 5 minutes for well done. Transfer the patties to a plate to rest for 5 minutes.

4 Return the pan to a medium heat and add the onions. Pour in the stock, bring to a simmer and add the remaining 1 teaspoon soy sauce. Whisk in the cornflour mixture and simmer for about 1 minute until the sauce is lightly thickened. Taste to adjust the seasoning with salt and pepper, if necessary.

5 Break the eggs into a bowl. Heat a medium non-stick sauté pan over a medium heat. Add 1 tablespoon of the oil, and when hot, gently slide in the eggs. Cook for about 1 minute, turn and cook for about 2 minutes until the whites are set and the yolks are still soft. (If you prefer your eggs sunny side up, add the eggs, cover and cook for about 1 minute, then uncover and cook for 2–3 minutes until the whites are set and the yolks are still soft.) Season with salt and pepper.

6 Divide the rice between 4 soup plates or serving bowls, top with the burgers and then top with the onions. With a non-metal spatula, separate the eggs, transfer to the onions, garnish with the reserved spring onion greens and serve.

To Drink:
A chilled lager like Yanjing

Ming's tips:

Most people like their burgers on the rare side, but for this dish, rare or well done work equally well. For tender burgers, form the patties as lightly as possible. Then, to ensure even cooking, make an indentation with your thumb halfway into the centre of each.

To avoid contamination from cutlery, crack the eggs against the side of a work surface, or against one another. The method for making the eggs – pouring all the eggs from a bowl into the hot pan and, when cooked, separating them with a spatula – is good to know when preparing fried eggs for a crowd.

The first person to stuff a pepper was a genius. While flavourful, most peppers taste pretty much the same – it's the stuffing that makes the difference. Here, peppers are filled with a savoury mixture of sausagemeat plus spicy fried rice, an Asian touch that makes the dish soar. Served on a bed of spinach dressed with lemon juice, these make a perfect family supper.

PEPPERS STUFFED WITH SPICY PORK FRIED RICE

SERVES 4

4 large red peppers
5 tablespoons rapeseed (canola) oil, plus extra for coating the peppers
Sea salt and freshly ground black pepper
4 large eggs, beaten
450g spicy Italian pork sausagemeat (or remove the meat from the skins of fresh spicy Italian pork sausages or other good-quality spicy pork sausages)
1 tablespoon finely chopped fresh ginger
1 tablespoon finely chopped garlic
1 jalapeño chilli, finely chopped
2 bunches spring onions, white and green parts separated, thinly sliced, 3 tablespoons of the greens reserved for garnish
700g cooked 50-50 White and Brown Rice (page 13)
1 tablespoon wheat-free tamari
225g baby spinach leaves
Juice of 1 lemon

1 Preheat the oven to 180°C/fan 160°C/Gas Mark 4. Remove the stems from the peppers and cut off the tops. Finely chop the tops and set aside. Remove the pepper seeds and ribs. Coat the peppers inside and out with oil, season with salt and pepper and transfer to a baking dish. Bake for 10–12 minutes until the peppers have softened.

2 Cover a large dish with kitchen paper. Season the eggs with salt and pepper. Heat a large sauté pan over a high heat. Add 4 tablespoons of the oil and swirl to coat the pan. When the oil is almost smoking, add the eggs and cook, stirring constantly, for about 15 seconds until scrambled. Transfer the eggs to the kitchen paper to drain.

3 In the same pan and over a medium-high heat, sauté the sausagemeat, breaking it up, for 6–8 minutes until cooked through. Transfer to a medium plate and set aside.

4 Return the pan to a medium-high heat. Add the remaining 1 tablespoon oil and swirl to coat the pan. When the oil is hot, add the ginger, garlic, jalapeño and all but the reserved spring onion greens. Season with salt and pepper. Add the rice, tamari, eggs, sausagemeat and reserved finely chopped peppers and heat through, stirring, for 2–3 minutes. Adjust the seasoning if necessary.

5 In a medium bowl, combine the spinach with the lemon juice, season with salt and pepper and toss. Divide the spinach between 4 plates. Stuff the peppers with the rice mixture. Place on top of the beds of spinach, garnish with the spring onion greens and serve.

To Drink:
Yanjing or Sapporo Premium beer

Pork with fruit is a natural combo, and one that appears in many cultures. The Chinese have sweet and sour pork with pineapple, for example, and Brits and Americans alike enjoy pork with apple sauce. For this easy pork chop dish I've upped the ante by combining dried fruit – cranberries – with fresh, tart apples. I've also added a hash made from nature's most nutritious spud, the sweet potato, so the dish really takes off.

PORK CHOPS
with Dried Cranberry–Apple Sweet Potato Hash

SERVES 4

1 tablespoon paprika
1 teaspoon ground ginger
1 tablespoon granulated sugar
1 tablespoon sea salt, plus extra for seasoning
4 large thick loin or spare rib pork chops
3 tablespoons rapeseed (canola) oil
1 large red onion, cut into 1cm dice
1 tablespoon finely chopped fresh ginger
2 large sweet potatoes, peeled and cut into 2.5cm pieces
Freshly ground back pepper
120g dried cranberries
2 Granny Smith apples, peeled, cored and cut into 2.5cm pieces
120ml dark rum

1 Preheat the oven to 200°C/fan 180°C/Gas Mark 6. First make the rub. In a small bowl, combine the paprika, ground ginger, sugar and 1 tablespoon salt. Blend and rub well into the chops. Set aside in the refrigerator for 4 hours.

2 Heat a large ovenproof sauté pan over a medium-high heat. Add 2 tablespoons of the oil and swirl to coat the pan. When the oil is hot, add the chops and cook on for about 1 minute per side until browned. Remove the chops and set aside.

3 Add the remaining 1 tablespoon oil and swirl to coat the pan. When the oil is hot, add the onion, fresh ginger and sweet potatoes, season with salt and pepper and sauté, stirring, for 3 minutes. Add the dried cranberries, apples and rum and flambé. Top with the chops and transfer the pan to the oven. Roast for 10–12 minutes until the pork is cooked but still pink in the centre, or to 57°C on a meat thermometer. Bring to the table in the pan and serve.

Ming's tips:

Don't buy pork chops with a set idea about getting a loin or spare rib cut. Instead, go by which looks best.

To flambé the rum using a gas flame, avert your face and tilt the pan into the gas. Over an electric burner, allow the rum to heat, then ignite it with a long kitchen match or an automatic lighter.

To Drink:

A bright young Pinot Noir or chilled Gamay Beaujolais like Laboure-Roi Beaujolais-Villages Saint Armand

In an outdoor restaurant in Morocco I had an awesome dish of boned lamb shoulder cooked over coals and served with a mountain of couscous. It inspired this super-spicy version that features couscous made traditionally – steamed over cooking meat. Besides providing subtle flavour, steaming gives couscous a wonderful fluffy texture. I love lamb shoulder. It has luscious pockets of fat that flavour the meat as it braises. This is a perfect dish to serve to food-loving friends.

BRAISED 8-SPICE LAMB SHOULDER
with Couscous

SERVES 4

525g traditional (not quick-cook) couscous

1.1kg trimmed lamb shoulder, cut into 2.5cm cubes

Sea salt

Rapeseed (canola) oil for searing the meat

2 large onions, cut into 2.5cm pieces

Cloves from 1 head garlic, peeled and smashed

450g baby carrots

1 bunch celery, sticks cut into 2.5cm lengths

1 banana, peeled

RUB

1 tablespoon ground coriander

1 tablespoon ground cumin

1 tablespoon freshly ground black pepper

1 tablespoon paprika

1 tablespoon cayenne pepper

1 tablespoon ground ginger

1 tablespoon ground fennel seeds

1 tablespoon ground cinnamon

To Drink:

A Rhone GSM, like JL Colombo Les Abielles Côtes du Rhone Rouge

1 Put the couscous in a large bowl. Add room-temperature water to cover and leave to stand for 30 minutes. Set aside.

2 For the rub, in a small bowl, combine the coriander, cumin, pepper, paprika, cayenne, ginger, fennel and cinnamon and mix together.

3 Season the lamb with salt and coat with the rub. (You may not need it all. Save any extra for seasoning steak or chicken.)

4 Heat a large saucepan or flameproof casserole dish over a high heat. Add 2 tablespoons of the oil and swirl to coat the base. When the oil is hot, and working in batches, add the meat and sear on all sides for about 6 minutes just until coloured. Wipe out the pan between batches to avoid burning the spices and use extra oil for each batch. Transfer the meat to a large plate.

5 Without wiping out the pan, add the onions, garlic, carrots and celery and season with salt and pepper. Sauté over a medium-high heat, stirring, for 2 minutes. Return the meat with its juices to the pan and add enough water to almost cover it. Adjust the seasoning if necessary, add the banana and bring to a simmer. Cover and cook for 30 minutes.

6 Meanwhile, line a colander or steamer basket that will fit into the pan with muslin and place the couscous in it. When the meat has cooked for 30 minutes, fit the colander into the top of the pan and cover with foil, crimping it tightly around the pan edge to avoid steam escaping. Simmer for 1–1¼ hours until the meat is tender and the couscous is cooked. If the banana hasn't disintegrated, mash it into the liquid. Transfer the couscous to a large deep platter, top with the lamb and serve with bowls of broth.

Ming's tip:
If you have a sturdy metal steamer, by all means use it to braise the meat and steam the couscous.

Our Blue Ginger Burger, which has gained some fame in the burger wars, is packed with umami – that savoury 'fifth taste' present in cheese and mushrooms, among other ingredients. Specifically, the burger contains a Parmesan and shiitake tuile – delicious, but laborious to make. Here's my easy-to-do version that keeps the cheese and mushrooms in the burger and also features a spicy mayo spread. Serve these with your favourite crisps.

SHIITAKE AND PARMESAN HAMBURGER

SERVES 4

3 tablespoons rapeseed (canola) oil
2 large shallots, finely chopped
450g shiitake mushrooms, stems
 removed, roughly chopped
Sea salt and freshly ground
 black pepper
900g beef mince
100g Parmesan cheese, grated
4 tablespoons Dijon mustard
3 tablespoons mayonnaise
4 dashes sriracha or other hot sauce
 like Frank's or Tabasco sauce
4 best-quality burger buns
1 head iceberg lettuce, shredded
1 large tomato, cut into 5mm slices

1 Heat a large sauté pan over a medium-high heat. Add 1 tablespoon of the oil and swirl to coat the pan. When the oil is hot, add the shallots and sweat them for 30 seconds–1 minute, then add the shiitakes. Season with salt and pepper and sauté, stirring, for about 4 minutes until the shiitakes are soft. Set aside to cool. Reserve the pan.

2 Meanwhile, in a medium bowl, combine the meat with the Parmesan. When the mushroom mixture is cool, add to the meat and mix lightly. Gently form into 4 burgers and season with salt and pepper. Heat the pan over a medium-high heat. Add the remaining 2 tablespoons oil and swirl to coat the pan. When the oil is hot, add the burgers and cook for about 4 minutes. Turn the burgers, lower the heat to medium-low and continue to cook for 5–6 minutes for medium-rare.

3 Meanwhile, in a small bowl, combine the mustard, mayonnaise and sriracha. Toast the buns and spread the mustard mixture on both crumb sides. Top the bottom halves with the shredded lettuce and add the burgers. Season the tomato slices with salt and pepper and place on top of the burgers. Top with the remaining bun halves and serve.

Ming's tips:

Remember to form the burgers lightly, compressing them only until the meat coheres. And don't press them with a spatula as they cook, which can force juices into the pan.

If tomatoes aren't in season, omit them rather than using inferior specimens.

Video tip:

Watch the video for my simple technique for chopping shallots.

To Drink:
Yanjing beer or a Pinot Noir

This was inspired by the classic Italian dish veal Marsala. But instead of the usual mushrooms, I use meaty shiitakes, and port in place of the traditional fortified wine. The bigger news is that I sub pork for the veal – blame it on my Chinese ancestry. Besides being cheaper than veal, pork, with its luscious fat, is really terrific in this dish. The panko makes a particularly delicate crust – I recommend it for most breading. This is a great dinner party dish.

PANKO-CRUSTED PORK CUTLETS
with Mushroom Sauce

SERVES 4

900g boneless pork loin, cut into
  4 equal pieces
125g wholemeal or white
  plain flour
3 large eggs
120g panko breadcrumbs
4 tablespoons chopped parsley, plus
  extra for garnish
2 lemons, the juice of 1, the zest of 2
Sea salt and freshly ground
  black pepper
5 tablespoons rapeseed (canola) oil
2 large shallots, thinly sliced
450g mushrooms, thinly sliced
240ml ruby port or dry sherry
360ml fresh chicken stock or
  low-sodium bought
½ tablespoon cornflour mixed with
  ½ tablespoon cold water

1 Preheat the oven to 120°C/fan 100°C/Gas Mark ½. Put the pork on a large chopping board and cover with a doubled-up sheet of cling film. Using a mallet or heavy small sauté pan, pound the pork to a thickness of about 3mm.

2 Put the flour, eggs and panko in separate shallow dishes. Beat the eggs until well combined. Add the parsley and half the lemon zest to the panko and stir to blend.

3 Season the pork lightly on both sides with salt and pepper. Dredge the pork in the flour, dip in the egg and drain the excess, then dredge in the panko. Transfer to a large plate.

4 Heat a large frying pan or sauté pan over a medium-high heat. Add 2 tablespoons of the oil and swirl to coat the pan. When the oil is hot, and working in 2 batches with 2 more tablespoons oil, add the pork and sauté, turning once, for about 3 minutes per side until golden. As each cutlet is done, transfer it to a plate and keep warm in the oven. Repeat with the remaining pork.

5 Wipe out the pan and heat over a high heat. Add the remaining 1 tablespoon oil and swirl to coat the pan. When the oil is hot, add the shallots and sauté, without stirring, for about 3 minutes until soft. Add the mushrooms and sauté, stirring, for about 2 minutes until browned. Add the port and lemon juice, stir and simmer for about 1 minute until the liquid is reduced by half. Add the stock and bring to a simmer. Whisk in 1 teaspoon of the cornflour mixture and simmer for about 1 minute until lightly thickened. Adjust the seasoning, if necessary.

6 Transfer the mushroom mixture to a rimmed serving platter and top with the cutlets. Garnish with the extra parsley and remaining zest and serve.

To Drink:

A New World Pinot Noir, like
Veramonte Ritual, from Chile

Ming's tip:

When cooking a whole pork shoulder, I would brine the meat to keep in the moisture. But as these are smaller cutlets, no brining is necessary.

Video tip:

Watch the video to learn my simple technique for chopping fresh parsley.

Not every curry is Indian or contains curry powder. Curries are made throughout Southeast Asia, and can include all sorts of spicy ingredients, wet and dry. Case in point, this terrific Thai-influenced red curry that owes its colour to chilli powder and paprika. Carrots and sweet potatoes add contrast to its heat, as does the coconut milk, and the pork itself. This is very easy to put together for a quick weeknight meal.

RED CURRY BRAISED PORK ON RICE

SERVES 4

3 tablespoons rapeseed (canola) oil, plus extra if needed

900g pork shoulder, trimmed and cut into 2.5cm cubes

Sea salt and freshly ground black pepper

2 large onions, cut into 2.5cm pieces

1 tablespoon finely chopped fresh ginger

2 red or green jalapeño chillies, finely chopped

1 tablespoon chilli powder

1 tablespoon paprika

450g baby carrots

2 large sweet potatoes, peeled and cut into 2.5cm dice

240ml unsweetened coconut milk

1 bay leaf

Juice of 1 lime

1kg cooked 50-50 White and Brown Rice (page 13)

1 Heat a large saucepan over a medium-high heat. Add 2 tablespoons of the oil and swirl to coat the base. When the oil is hot, and working in batches with additional oil if necessary, add the pork, season with salt and pepper and cook for 4–6 minutes until coloured on all sides. Transfer the pork to a plate.

2 To the same pan, add the remaining 1 tablespoon oil and swirl to coat the base. Add the onions, ginger and jalapeños and sauté over a medium-high heat, stirring, for about 5 minutes until the onions are lightly browned. Add the chilli powder and paprika and sauté, stirring, for 30 seconds. Add the carrots, sweet potatoes, coconut milk and bay leaf, then add water to cover the vegetables by 2.5cm. Adjust the seasoning, if necessary, and return the pork to the pan. If the pork isn't completely covered, add more water. Bring to a simmer, cover and cook for about 1½ hours until the pork is tender. Remove the bay leaf, add the lime juice and stir, then serve with the rice.

Ming's tip:

You can make this dish in a pressure cooker to save time. Follow the instructions up to the final braising and lock the lid in place according to the manufacturer's instructions. When the steam begins to hiss out of the cooker, reduce the heat to low, just enough to maintain a very weak whistle, and cook for 45 minutes.

Video tip:

Watch the video to see me cook this dish in a pressure cooker.

To Drink:

A Riesling like Weingut Johann Haart Piesporter Treppchen

This began as a squab (young pigeon) dish. Then I got the idea to use an equally full-flavoured meat, lamb mince, instead. This in turn proposed the sambal yogurt accompaniment, a delicious Asian–Greek mix. Apricots sweeten the sautéed lamb, which is served in crisp lettuce cups. In short, this is a terrific medley of contrasting flavours, textures and even temperatures, given the cooling yogurt.

APRICOT LAMB LETTUCE CUPS
with Sambal Yogurt

SERVES 4

55g flaked almonds
1 tablespoon sambal or other chilli paste
240g fat-free natural Greek yogurt
95g dried apricots, preferably unsulphured, chopped
1 bunch spring onions, white and greens parts separated, thinly sliced
1 tablespoon rapeseed (canola) oil
450g lamb mince
Sea salt and freshly ground black pepper
1 tablespoon ground coriander
1 tablespoon finely chopped garlic
2 large leeks, white parts, cut into 1cm dice (see Tip)
110g peeled carrot, grated
Palm-size leaves from 1 head iceberg lettuce

To Drink:
A Côte du Rhone or GSM blend, like Gran Clos Finca el Puig Priorat from Spain

1 Heat a small sauté pan over a medium-high heat. Add the almonds and toast, stirring, for 1–2 minutes. Transfer to a plate and set aside.

2 In a medium bowl, combine the sambal, yogurt, apricots and spring onion greens. Mix and set aside.

3 Heat a wok or large sauté pan over a high heat. Add the oil and swirl to coat the pan. When the oil is hot, add the lamb and sauté, breaking up the meat, for 3–4 minutes until it loses its colour. Add the coriander and continue to sauté, stirring, for 3–4 minutes until the lamb is cooked through. With a slotted spoon, transfer the meat to a plate.

4 Add the garlic, leeks and spring onion whites to the pan, season with salt and pepper and cook over a medium heat, stirring occasionally, for 4–5 minutes until the vegetables are soft but not coloured. Add the carrots and lamb to the pan. Stir and heat through for about 2 minutes.

5 Transfer the lettuce cups to a platter or plates. Fill the cups with the lamb mixture and garnish with the almonds. Serve with the yogurt dolloped on top or on the side.

Ming's tip:

To dice the leeks easily, remove most of the green parts, leaving a bit attached to the white, and trim the root ends. Slice the leeks vertically, without cutting into the green ends. Turn the leeks and slice, then turn and slice again so that each leek has been cut into sixths. Fill a salad spinner bowl with water. Cut the white parts of the leeks into 1cm dice, transfer to the water and swish with your hands to remove any sand. Pour the leeks with the water into the spinner insert, rinse the leeks under running water to remove any transferred grit and spin the leeks dry.

CHAPTER 5

Poultry

Everyone loves chicken. It's versatile, affordable and tasty. My challenge is to use it in fresh ways – either by recasting traditional recipes or creating something new.

For old-into-new, I offer Best-Ever Roast Chicken with Gingered Sweet Potatoes, a luscious pairing of the bird with sweets that are roasted with it, and Wok-Stirred Chilli 'n' Cashew Chicken, my fiery, cashew-laced take on kung pao chicken and a great family dish. Crispy Wings in Sweet Chilli Sauce will become your default wing dish – and for the best, moistest meatloaf ever, I present Chicken–Onion Meatloaf with Sambal–Worcestershire Gravy, made super flavourful with dark chicken meat.

As for 'new', you can't do better than Soy–Sake Roasted Chicken 'n' Eggs, a pairing of braised eggs, a traditional Chinese favourite, and roast chicken legs and thighs. A totally special dish, this delights guests.

I don't neglect other birds. Turkey Scaloppini with Black Bean–Onion Sauce and Spinach makes use of convenient turkey breast for the scaloppini, and is the best reason I know to serve the bird often. Pan-Roasted Duck Breast with Mushroom Fricassée pairs luscious duck breast with shiitakes and oyster mushrooms, a deeply satisfying marriage. It's yet another reason to enjoy birds, and for all occasions.

One of my fondest Paris memories is of the street aroma of cooking rotisserie chickens. Your nose often makes eating decisions for you, and I enjoyed *lots* of those chickens there. Normally, we can't make rotisserie chicken at home, but roasting is a wonderful way to duplicate rotisserie savour. And what's better than serving the roasted bird with sweet potatoes that have cooked in its delicious fat? Nothing!

BEST-EVER ROAST CHICKEN
with Gingered Sweet Potatoes

SERVES 6

55g sea salt, for brining,
    plus more to season

65g granulated sugar

1 x 2.7–3.6kg chicken

3 tablespoons extra-virgin olive oil

2 tablespoons finely chopped garlic

2 tablespoons finely chopped fresh
    thyme

Freshly ground black pepper

1 tablespoon finely chopped fresh
    ginger

2 tablespoons light agave syrup or
    runny honey

3 large sweet potatoes, peeled and cut
    into 2.5cm pieces

1 bunch spring onions, white and green
    parts, thinly sliced

To Drink:

An unoaked Chardonnay, like
Qupé Bien Nacido 'y' Block,
from California

1 The day before, brine the chicken. In a large jug, combine the 55g salt and the sugar with 1.9 litres water and stir to dissolve the sugar and salt. Put the chicken in a bowl or pan large enough to hold it and the brine and pour the brine over the chicken. If the chicken isn't covered, make more brine and add it to the bowl. Refrigerate overnight. Rinse the chicken and pat dry.

2 Preheat the oven to 240°C/fan 220°C/Gas 9. Place a roasting pan on the middle oven shelf and heat.

3 Rub the chicken inside and out with 2 tablespoons olive oil, the garlic and 1 tablespoon of the thyme. Season with salt and pepper inside and out.

4 In a large bowl, combine the ginger, syrup, sweet potatoes, spring onions, the remaining 1 tablespoon thyme and the remaining 1 tablespoon oil. Mix well and season with salt and pepper.

5 Pull out the oven shelf with the pan and add the vegetables, which will sizzle. Top with the chicken, breast side up, and roast for 15 to 20 minutes. Lower the oven temperature to 190°C/fan 170°C/Gas Mark 5 and continue to roast, turning the pan once front to back and stirring the potatoes halfway through cooking, for 1¼ hours longer until the chicken is done, or until the chicken registers an internal temperature of 70°C on a meat thermometer. If the chicken is colouring too quickly, tent it with foil. Remove the foil tent 10 minutes before the chicken is cooked so that the skin crisps.

6 Transfer the chicken to a chopping board to rest for 10 minutes. Transfer the sweet potatoes to a platter. Carve the chicken, place on top of the potatoes, spoon pan juices over the chicken and serve.

Kung pao chicken, the spicy, peanut-garnished Hunan dish, is a great family fave. I love peanuts, but for this dish I love cashews more, and you will too. Traditional 'kung pao' is usually made with chicken breast; I use skinless thigh meat, which is much more flavourful but has about the same calories as the white meat. This delicious dish is also very easy on the pocket.

WOK-STIRRED CHILLI 'N' CASHEW CHICKEN

SERVES 4

4 tablespoons rapeseed (canola) oil

140g salted roasted cashew nuts

1 teaspoon cayenne pepper, or to taste

1 tablespoon runny honey

900g boneless, skinless chicken thighs, cut into 1cm pieces

Sea salt and freshly ground black pepper

2 jalapeño or serrano chillies with seeds, thinly sliced

1 large onion, cut into 1cm pieces

1 large red pepper, cut into 1cm pieces

60ml white wine or fresh chicken stock or low-sodium bought

2 tablespoons vegetarian oyster sauce

700g cooked 50-50 White and Brown Rice (page 13)

1 Heat a wok or large sauté pan over a high heat. Add 1 tablespoon of the oil and swirl to coat the pan. When the oil is hot, add the cashews and fry, stirring, for 30 seconds until darkly coloured. Transfer the nuts to a medium bowl, add the cayenne and honey and stir. Set aside.

2 Heat the wok over a high heat. Add 2 tablespoons of the oil and swirl to coat the pan. When the oil is hot, add the chicken, season with salt and pepper and stir-fry for about 5 minutes until the chicken is cooked through. Transfer to a medium bowl and set aside.

3 Heat the wok over a high heat. Add the remaining 1 tablespoon oil and swirl to coat the pan. When the oil is hot, add the jalapeños and sauté, stirring, for 30 seconds. Add the onion and red pepper and stir-fry for about 2 minutes until softened. Return the chicken and all but 1 tablespoon of the cashews to the wok and add the wine. Add the oyster sauce, stir and adjust the seasoning, if necessary. Transfer to a platter.

4 Divide the rice between 4 rice bowls. Top with some of the stir-fry, reserving the rest for second helpings. Garnish with the reserved cashews and serve.

Ming's tip:

Lightly frying already roasted cashews releases more of their flavour.

Video tip:

Watch the video to learn my simple technique for rolling and chopping peppers.

To Drink:

A Riesling, like Domaines Schlumberger 'Les Princes Abbés'

People should enjoy turkey year-long. You don't have to roast a whole one – its breast is a delicious and convenient route to easy turkey dinners. Like chicken breast, though, it can be dry. That's avoided in this delicious recipe by cutting the breast into scaloppini, breading them with tarragon-flavoured panko and then sautéeing them until golden – a great way to add flavour as well as sealing in juices. The black bean–onion sauce is a great accompaniment, and the spinach 'side' adds its own great taste.

TURKEY SCALOPPINI
with Black Bean–Onion Sauce and Spinach

SERVES 4

125g wholemeal or white plain flour
3 large eggs
120g panko breadcrumbs
2 tablespoons finely chopped fresh
  tarragon
1 x 1.3–1.8kg boneless, skinless
  turkey breast
Sea salt and freshly ground
  black pepper
5 tablespoons rapeseed (canola) oil
1 tablespoon extra-virgin olive oil
1 bag (250–280g) baby
  spinach leaves, stems removed,
  washed and spun dry
Zest and juice of 2 lemons,
  2 teaspoons zest reserved for
  garnish
1 large onion, finely chopped
1 tablespoon finely chopped
  fermented black beans
480ml fresh chicken stock or
  low-sodium bought
25g unsalted butter

To Drink:

A chilled Gamay like Louis Latour
Beaujolais Villages

1 Preheat the oven to 120°C/fan 100°C/Gas Mark ½.

2 Put the flour, eggs and panko in separate shallow dishes. Add the tarragon to the panko and stir to blend.

3 Remove the tenderloin from the turkey breast (reserve it for another use) and cut the meat on the extreme bias into 2.5cm-thick cutlets. Place the cutlets on a chopping board, cover with cling film and, using a mallet or small sauté pan, pound the cutlets until about 3mm thick. Season the turkey on both sides with salt and pepper. Dredge the turkey in the flour, dip in the egg and drain the excess, then dredge in the panko. Transfer to a large plate.

4 Heat a large frying pan over a medium-high heat. Add 2 tablespoons of the rapeseed (canola) oil and swirl to coat the pan. When the oil is hot, add half the turkey scaloppini and sear, turning once, for about 3 minutes per side until brown and cooked through. Repeat with another 2 tablespoons oil and the remaining scaloppini. Transfer the turkey to a baking sheet and keep warm in the oven.

5 Wipe out the pan and return it to a high heat. Add the olive oil and swirl to coat the pan. When the oil is hot, add the spinach and lemon zest and sauté, stirring, for 30 seconds. Season with salt and pepper and sauté, stirring, for about a further 1 minute until the spinach has wilted. Transfer to a medium bowl.

6 Wipe out the pan and heat over a high heat. Add the remaining 1 tablespoon rapeseed (canola) oil and swirl to coat the pan. When the oil is hot, add the onion and black beans and sauté, stirring, for about 2 minutes until the onion is lightly coloured. Season with salt and pepper. Add the lemon juice and stock, bring to a simmer and cook for about 5 minutes until the liquid is reduced by half. Whisk in the butter.

7 Transfer the spinach to a platter and top with the turkey. Spoon the pan sauce around, garnish with the reserved lemon zest, and serve.

Video tip:

Watch the video to see me prepare the turkey breast.

After years of operation, my mum sold our family restaurant, Mandarin Kitchen, to a Korean couple. The new owners put crispy chicken wings on the menu, which they served with a sweet–spicy, garlicky sauce. I ate a lot of that fabulous dish and begged for the sauce recipe, but I could never get it. When I became a chef, one of my priorities was to reproduce the dish – and here it is, a Blue Ginger favourite. The wings are fantastic for parties and other gatherings. Just make more than you think you'll need, as they disappear fast.

CRISPY WINGS IN SWEET CHILLI SAUCE

SERVES 4

3 tablespoons rapeseed (canola) oil, plus extra for frying

2 red onions, roughly chopped

1 tablespoon finely chopped garlic

2 red or green jalapeño chillies, finely chopped

Sea salt and freshly ground black pepper

2 red peppers, deseeded and roughly chopped

240ml rice vinegar

4 tablespoons light agave syrup or honey

1.3kg chicken wings, drummette and wing ends separated, washed and patted dry

2 tablespoons toasted sesame seeds

1 Heat a medium sauté pan over a medium-high heat. Add 1 tablespoon of the oil and swirl to coat the pan. When the pan is hot, add the onions and garlic and sauté, stirring, for 1 minute. Add the jalapeños, season with salt and black pepper and sauté for about 8 minutes until soft. Add the red peppers and sauté, stirring, for about 2 minutes until softened. Add the vinegar, stir and sauté for about 5 minutes until the liquid is reduced by half. Transfer the mixture to a blender and purée, drizzling in the syrup and the remaining 2 tablespoons oil. Season with salt and pepper and continue to purée until the mixture is very smooth. Set aside.

2 Half-fill a large heavy saucepan with oil. Heat over a high heat to 190°–200°C on a deep-frying thermometer. Cover a platter with kitchen paper.

3 Season the wings with salt and pepper. Working in batches, if necessary, add the wings to the oil gradually, and fry for 20–25 minutes until they are crisp and golden. Transfer to the kitchen paper to drain, then to a large serving bowl. Add half the sesame seeds and some of the sauce to coat the wings lightly. Garnish with the remaining sesame seeds and serve with the remaining sauce on the side.

To Drink:

Chilled beer, like Sam Adams lager

Everyone loves meatloaf – when it's done right. This meatloaf recipe features dark chicken meat, which not only delivers great taste but is better for you than the usual beef. The gravy is flavoured with Worcestershire, an underused condiment that's a tart foil for the sambal. I often make this dish just for the leftovers – a sandwich of the sliced loaf on toasted bread with crisp lettuce and hot Dijon mustard will make you very, very happy.

CHICKEN-ONION MEATLOAF
with Sambal-Worcestershire Gravy

SERVES 4

1 tablespoon plus 1 teaspoon rapeseed (canola) oil, plus extra for oiling the loaf tin

3 large onions, diced

Sea salt and freshly ground black pepper

2 tablespoons finely chopped garlic

900g minced dark chicken meat or good-quality chicken mince

175g cooked brown or white long-grain rice

30g chopped parsley, plus about 12 leaves for garnish

240g celery sticks, diced

1 tablespoon sambal or other chilli seasoning

60ml organic Worcestershire sauce

480ml fresh chicken stock or low-sodium bought

1 tablespoon cornflour mixed with 1 tablespoon water

1 Preheat the oven to 180°C/fan 160°C/Gas Mark 4. Oil a 13cm × 23cm loaf tin.

2 Heat a large sauté pan over a medium-high heat. Add 1 tablespoon oil and swirl to coat the pan. When the oil is hot, add the onions and season with salt and pepper. Add the garlic and sauté, stirring, for about 10 minutes until caramelised. Transfer two-thirds of the mixture to a large bowl and let cool.

3 Add the chicken, rice and parsley, blend, and season with salt and pepper. Test the seasoning by sautéeing 1 tablespoon of the mixture in a little hot oil or in a microwave for 20 seconds on high power. Adjust the seasoning with salt and pepper, if necessary.

4 Transfer the mixture to the tin without packing it tightly and pat the top smooth. Bake for about 45 minutes until cooked through, or until a knife inserted in the middle of the loaf comes out clean. Leave to stand for 10 minutes, then unmould and slice. Transfer the slices to a platter or individual plates.

5 Meanwhile, heat the sauté pan with the remaining onion mixture over a medium-high heat. Add the 1 teaspoon of oil and swirl to coat the pan. Add the celery, season with salt and pepper, and sauté, stirring, for about 3 minutes until soft. Add the sambal, Worcestershire sauce, stock and meat juices, bring to a simmer and cook for 3–4 minutes to reduce by one-quarter. Whisk in three-quarters of the cornflour mixture in a thin stream, season with salt and pepper and simmer for about 3 minutes until lightly thickened. Spoon the sauce over the meatloaf, garnish with the parsley leaves, and serve.

Ming's tip:
The recipe instructs you to test the loaf mixture for seasoning by cooking a bit of it. This may seem fussy, but it's really necessary to ensure best flavour.

To Drink:
A spicy California Zinfandel

The first time I had pineapple fried rice was in Hawaii. It was made by restaurateur and chef Sam Choy, and contained Spam. I had my doubts about that popular Hawaiian ingredient, but the dish was delicious, and is the inspiration for this version, which features chicken sausagemeat rather than Spam. The spicy chicken is a perfect match for the fresh pineapple, and the whole dish a satisfying meal in one.

CHICKEN SAUSAGE FRIED RICE
with Pineapple

SERVES 4

2 tablespoons rapeseed (canola) oil

675g chicken sausagemeat, preferably Italian

1 cucumber, very thinly sliced (see Tip, page 67)

Juice and zest of 1 lemon

1 teaspoon toasted sesame oil

Sea salt and freshly ground black pepper

5 garlic cloves, sliced as thinly as possible

1 tablespoon finely chopped fresh ginger

1 bunch spring onions, white and green parts, thinly sliced, 2 tablespoons of the greens reserved for garnish

1 tablespoon sambal

½ pineapple, peeled, cored and diced

1 large red pepper, diced

1kg 50-50 White and Brown Rice, cooked and cooled (page 13)

1 tablespoon wheat-free tamari

1 Heat a wok over a high heat. Add 1 tablespoon of the rapeseed (canola) oil and swirl to coat the pan. When the oil is hot, add the sausagemeat and sauté, breaking up the meat, for 6–8 minutes until cooked through. Transfer to a plate.

2 In a medium bowl, combine the cucumber, lemon juice and zest and sesame oil. Season with salt and black pepper and set aside.

3 Heat the wok over a high heat. Add the remaining 1 tablespoon rapeseed (canola) oil and swirl to coat the pan. When the oil is hot, add the garlic, ginger, spring onions and sambal and sauté, stirring, for 30 seconds until fragrant. Add the pineapple and red pepper and sauté until the rawness is cooked out, about 1 minute. Add the rice and tamari, season with pepper, and heat through, stirring, for 1 minute. Return the sausagemeat to the pan and heat through, stirring occasionally. Taste and adjust the seasoning with salt and pepper, if necessary.

4 Transfer the rice to a large serving bowl. Top with the cucumber mixture, garnish with the spring onion greens and serve.

To Drink:

A Pinot Blanc, like Trimbach

Duck breast is underused by many cooks. That's a shame, as it's easily prepared – you cook it just like steak – and wonderfully tasty. You also get the bonus of its deliciously crisp skin. Here, the sautéed breasts are paired with a fricassée made from potatoes that are cooked in the duck fat plus oyster and shiitake mushrooms. This is great eating, and pleases diners of every stripe.

PAN-ROASTED DUCK BREAST
with Mushroom Fricassée

SERVES 4

4 duck breasts (about 280g each), preferably Pekin or Gressingham, tenderloin, any sinew and excess fat removed

Sea salt and freshly ground black pepper

2 large Yukon Gold or Estima potatoes, peeled and cut into 1cm dice

2 shallots, finely chopped

1 tablespoon finely chopped garlic

350g shiitake mushrooms, stems removed, cut into 5mm-thick slices

60ml dry red wine

350g oyster mushrooms, stems trimmed, large ones torn into 4 pieces, smaller ones torn in half

1 bunch chives, cut into 3mm-thick slices, 1 tablespoon reserved for garnish

1 Score the skin side of the duck breasts in a crosshatch pattern, slicing only halfway through the fat layer.

2 Heat a large heavy sauté pan or cast-iron frying pan over a medium heat. Season the breasts with salt and pepper, turn the heat to low and cook, skin side down, for 20–25 minutes until brown and crisp. Transfer to a chopping board, skin side up, and set aside. Pour off all but 2 tablespoons of the fat into a heatproof bowl and reserve.

3 Return the pan to a medium-high heat. When the fat is hot, add the potatoes and season with salt and pepper. Cook, without stirring, for 3–4 minutes until browned. Turn over and brown the other side. Continue to turn and cook the potatoes for another 6–7 minutes until at least 3 sides are browned and the potatoes are cooked through. Transfer to a plate lined with kitchen paper and set aside.

4 Put 2 tablespoons of the reserved fat in the pan and swirl to coat. When the fat is hot, add the shallots and garlic, season with salt and pepper and sauté, stirring, for 1 minute. Add the shiitakes and sauté, stirring, for 1–2 minutes until softened. Add the wine and deglaze the pan. Add the oyster mushrooms, season with salt and pepper and sauté, stirring, for about 2 minutes until golden and cooked through. Adjust the seasoning. Return the potatoes to the pan and add all but the reserved chives. Stir, adjust the seasoning, if necessary, and transfer to a large platter.

5 Wipe out the pan and heat over a medium-high heat. Add 1 tablespoon fat and swirl to coat the pan. When the fat is hot, add the breasts meat side down and cook for 1–2 minutes until medium-rare. Flip over and cook for 1–2 minutes to re-crisp the skin sides. Transfer to a chopping board, slice and place on top of the potatoes. Garnish with the reserved chives and serve.

To Drink:

A French or Oregon Pinot Noir

Ming's tip:

I like to serve food on hot plates. To warm them easily, run under hot water for 30 seconds then dry them, or heat them in the microwave for 1 minute.

I'm a major fan of leeks, a vegetable I first discovered in France. Leeks are similar to spring onions, but have a delightfully sweet edge. They're paired here with dark chicken meat, carrots and homey mash made with luscious but low-cal Greek yogurt. You can see that this is a delicious, completely satisfying dish that works for weekend family dinners and company alike.

BRAISED CHICKEN AND LEEKS
on Country Mash

SERVES 4–6

5 large Yukon Gold or Estima
  potatoes, washed and dried
900g boneless, skinless chicken
  thighs, cut into 2.5cm pieces
Sea salt and freshly ground
  black pepper
4 tablespoons rapeseed (canola) oil
3 large leeks, white parts, halved,
  cut into strips, washed and dried
  (see Tip, page 114)
450g baby carrots
240ml white wine
2 heaped tablespoons fresh tarragon
  leaves, roughly chopped, plus extra
  leaves for garnish
2 tablespoons naturally brewed
  soy sauce
480ml fresh chicken stock or
  low-sodium bought, or water,
  plus more if needed
1 tablespoon cornflour mixed with
  1 tablespoon water
½ bunch spring onions, white and
  green parts, thinly sliced
490g fat-free natural Greek yogurt

1 Preheat the oven to 180°C/fan 160°C/Gas Mark 4. Wrap the potatoes in foil, pierce several times with a fork and bake for 45 minutes until soft.

2 Meanwhile, line a large plate with kitchen paper. Season the chicken with salt and pepper. Heat a large saucepan or flameproof casserole dish over a medium-high heat. Add 2 tablespoons of the oil and swirl to coat the pan. When the oil is hot, add the chicken and cook for 6–8 minutes until browned on all sides. Transfer the chicken to the kitchen paper and set aside.

3 In the same pan, over a medium-high heat, and the remaining 2 tablespoons oil and swirl to coat the pan. When the oil is hot, add the leeks and sauté, stirring, for 6–8 minutes until caramelised. Add the carrots, stir and season with salt and pepper. Add the wine, stir and simmer for about 1 minute until the liquid is reduced by one-quarter. Return the chicken to the pan and add the tarragon, soy sauce and stock. Bring to a simmer and adjust the seasoning with salt and pepper. Reduce the heat, cover and simmer for about 25 minutes until the chicken is cooked through. Turn the heat to high, whisk in the cornflour mixture and cook for about 30 seconds until thickened.

4 Transfer the potatoes to a large bowl and mash roughly with a masher or wooden spoon. Add the spring onions and mix well. Add 120ml of the braising liquid, and the yogurt, mix and season with salt and pepper.

5 Strike the reserved tarragon leaves with the heel of your hand to release their fragrance. Transfer the mash to serving bowls, top with the chicken, garnish with the tarragon leaves and serve.

To Drink:

A crisp French Chardonnay, like a Chablis from Simonnet Febvre

I'm known for my East-West cooking. This dish, however, draws on two Asian cuisines, Japanese and Chinese. The braising liquid contains soy and sake – the Japanese part – and the eggs, which are cracked and cooked in the liquid, are Chinese-inspired. Served with roasted chicken and a tasty slaw, the eggs are wonderfully flavoured and beautiful too – once shelled, they show a mosaic pattern made by the soy. As a kid, I enjoyed similar eggs for Easter while my friends ate the chocolate kind. Nobody envied my eggs, but once you taste their descendant in this terrific dish, you'll understand why I loved Easter.

SOY–SAKE ROASTED CHICKEN 'N' EGGS

SERVES 6

480ml naturally brewed soy sauce

480ml sake, preferably TY KU Silver

100g dark brown sugar

1 tablespoon finely chopped garlic

1 tablespoon finely chopped fresh
    ginger

6 chicken legs

6 chicken thighs

12 large eggs

2 bunches spring onions, white and
    green parts, cut into 1cm lengths

280g peeled carrots, grated

1 small head red cabbage,
    thinly sliced

Juice and zest of 2 lemons,
    1 teaspoon zest reserved
    for garnish

Freshly ground black pepper

1kg cooked 50-50 White and Brown
    Rice (page 13)

1 In a medium bowl, combine the soy sauce, sake, brown sugar, garlic and ginger and stir to combine. Reserve 120ml of the marinade and set aside. Put the chicken in a large bowl and pour the marinade over it. Turn the chicken to coat it evenly with the marinade, cover and refrigerate for 1 hour.

2 Fill a large bowl with ice and add water. Bring a large saucepan half-full of water to the boil. Add the eggs, cook for 3½ minutes and transfer to the bowl. When the eggs are cold, remove and crack the shells gently. Set aside. Dry the pan.

3 Preheat the oven to 200°C/fan 180°C/Gas Mark 6 and place a baking sheet large enough to hold all the chicken on the middle shelf. Drain the chicken, reserve the marinade and transfer the chicken to the baking sheet – the chicken will sizzle. Roast for about 35 minutes until cooked through, turning the chicken once. Glaze with the 120ml reserved marinade after 10 minutes, after the chicken is turned, and 5 minutes before it's cooked through.

4 In the meantime, add the remaining marinade to the pan and bring to a boil over a medium heat. Return the eggs to the pan, add the spring onions and carrots, cover and simmer over a low heat for 30 minutes. Using a slotted spoon, transfer the eggs to a medium bowl.

5 In a large bowl, combine the cabbage, lemon juice and all but the reserved zest, the cooked carrots and spring onions and toss. Leave to stand for 10 minutes.

6 Peel the eggs. Place a mound of the cabbage mixture in individual serving bowls. Top each with the chicken leg and thigh and 2 of the eggs. Garnish with the lemon zest and serve with bowls of the rice.

To Drink:

A chilled sake, like TY KU Silver

Say Japanese food and most people think sushi. But Japanese cooking is extremely diverse, and shares a number of dishes with other Asian cuisines. Curry is one common dish, as I discovered when I first went to a curry restaurant in Osaka. Japanese curries, which contain pork or chicken, are milder than the Indian kind and are served with rice. This Japanese curry features chicken served with rice and potatoes, which sounds like overkill, but is just right. An awesome cold-weather meal, this is also welcomed when the temperature has climbed.

JAPANESE CHICKEN CURRY
with Potatoes and Rice

SERVES 4

2 tablespoons rapeseed (canola) oil

2 large onions, cut into 1cm dice

2 tablespoons finely chopped fresh
    ginger

3 tablespoons curry powder,
    preferably Madras

Sea salt and freshly ground
    black pepper

900g boneless, skinless chicken
    thighs, cut into 2.5cm pieces

950 ml fresh chicken stock or low-
    sodium bought, or water

½ bunch celery, cut into
    2.5cm pieces

2 large Yukon Gold or Estima
    potatoes, peeled, squared and cut
    into 2.5cm cubes

4 tablespoons roughly chopped fresh
    flat-leaf parsley, half reserved for
    garnish

2 tablespoons cornflour mixed
    with 2 tablespoons cold water

1kg cooked 50-50 White and Brown
    Rice (page 13)

To Drink:

A lager or super clean-tasting
Japanese beer, like Sapporo

1 Heat a large saucepan over a medium-high heat. Add the oil and swirl to coat the base of the pan. When the oil is hot, add the onions and sweat for 3–4 minutes until soft and lightly coloured. Add the ginger and curry powder and sauté, stirring occasionally, for about 1 minute until aromatic. Season with salt and pepper.

2 Add the chicken, season with salt and pepper and add stock just to cover. Add the celery, potatoes and half the parsley and bring to a simmer. Taste to adjust the seasoning, if necessary. Set a cover ajar on the pot, lower the heat to medium-low and cook for about 45 minutes until the chicken is tender.

3 Turn the heat to high, whisk in the cornflour mixture and cook for about 1 minute until the liquid is thickened.

4 Divide the rice between plates. Top with the chicken, garnish with the reserved parsley and serve.

Video tips:

Watch the video to learn my simple technique for squaring and dicing potatoes, as well as how to prepare and add the cornflour mixture.

Everyone loves chicken pad Thai, Thailand's deliciously spicy noodle dish. The noodles used are rice sticks, which, besides being delightfully chewy, are gluten-free (for those allergic to it) and 'cooked' simply by soaking. My version is easier to make than many others – I've eliminated the traditional tamarind, which is hard to find and fussy to prepare – but nothing is lost in the flavour department, I promise. I include the traditional scrambled eggs, but you can omit them, if you like. You'll still have a wonderfully satisfying dish.

LEMONGRASS CHICKEN PAD THAI

SERVES 4–6

225g rice sticks
450g boneless, skinless chicken thighs, cut into strips about 3mm wide
Sea salt and freshly ground black pepper
3 tablespoons plus 1 teaspoon rapeseed (canola) oil
4 lemongrass stalks, white parts only, finely chopped (see Tip, page 166)
1 large red onion, thinly sliced
1 jalapeño chilli, cut into thin rings
3 large eggs, lightly beaten
1 large red pepper, deseeded and cut into 5mm-thick slices (see Tip)
2 tablespoons fish sauce
Juice and zest of 2 lemons

1 Place the noodles in a medium bowl and fill it with hot water to cover. Soak for 10–15 minutes until pliable but not completely soft. Drain and set aside.

2 Season the chicken with salt and black pepper. Heat a wok over a medium-high heat. Add 2 tablespoons of the oil and swirl to coat the pan. When the oil is hot, add the chicken and stir-fry for about 3 minutes until browned and cooked through. Set the chicken strips aside.

3 Return the wok to a medium-high heat. Add the remaining 1 tablespoon oil and swirl to coat. When the oil is hot, add the lemongrass, onion and jalapeño. Stir-fry for about 1 minute until the onion is soft. Push the mixture to one side of the wok, drizzle in the 1 teaspoon oil and add the eggs. Stir-fry, breaking up the eggs, for about 30 seconds until the eggs are cooked through. When the eggs are set, stir to incorporate the onion mixture.

4 Return the chicken to the pan, add the red peppers and stir. Add the fish sauce, lemon juice and zest and noodles. Stir and cook for about 2 minutes until heated through. Adjust the seasoning in necessary and transfer to a serving platter or plates and serve.

Ming's tips:

To slice the red pepper easily, first cut away both ends. Cut downwards into the pepper on one long side and 'peel' away its flesh by rolling the pepper while you cut. You'll have separated the useable part of the pepper from its core and seeds. Halve the useable part, stack the halves and slice lengthways.

The noodle-soaking method here, which uses hot water, is fairly quick. But, if you have more time, soak them in room temperature water for about 2 hours. Whichever method you choose, you're aiming for noodles that are soft but not mushy, as the noodles will continue to cook when heated through before serving.

To Drink:

A Riesling, like S A Prum, from Germany

CHAPTER 6

Vegetables, Rice and Noodles

In many cultures, especially Asian ones, grain and vegetable dishes rule. And rightfully so. Alone or combined, they can yield as much flavour, textural interest and satisfaction as meat dishes. They're also quick to make and usually lighter on the stomach and pocket than their meat cousins. When devising them, all you need is some imagination.

To spur inspiration, I often think wok. Three-Mushroom and Jicama Chow Mein, an exciting textural meld, and Wok-Stirred Courgettes and Onions with Black Garlic, which puts deeply flavourful black garlic centre stage, are wok-made in minutes. Another wok dish, Crazy Noodle Stir-Fry, is made with chewy rice noodles and seitan, a versatile, wheat-based product I endorse for its great texture and healthiness. Tofu is another great-for-you ingredient that, in its smoked version, shines in Singapore Curry Tofu Noodles and in Crispy Tofu with Peanut–Garlic Glaze, where it gets a hot-garlicky drizzle – totally delicious!

Couscous and vegetables are traditionally matched. I celebrate that pairing in Veggie Ragout with Couscous and Harissa Sauce, a deeply flavourful meld of aubergine, sweet potatoes and courgettes, among other ingredients. And rice lovers, which is most of us, will call Eight Treasure Fried Rice and Hunan Glazed Aubergine with Rice their new best friends. Grains and vegetables really open dining doors.

This began as a chicken-noodle stir-fry. Then I said to myself, Self, why not make this with seitan or tempeh instead of the poultry? Those wheat- and soya bean-based products have the look and texture of meat and, I soon found, work beautifully in this crazy-fiery dish, as does smoked tofu, another no-meat option. This isn't just for vegetarians; with its satisfying noodles and Thai-inspired flavours, it delights everyone.

CRAZY NOODLE STIR-FRY

SERVES 4

225g rice sticks

3 tablespoons rapeseed (canola) oil

1 large onion, finely chopped

1 tablespoon finely chopped garlic

1 tablespoon finely chopped fresh
 ginger

Sea salt and freshly ground
 black pepper

1 tablespoon sambal or hot sauce

3 large eggs, beaten

225g tempeh, crumbled, or seitan,
 pulsed in a food processor to the
 texture of minced meat

Juice of 2 limes

2 tablespoons naturally brewed
 soy sauce

1 red pepper, cut into 5mm-thick
 slices (see Tip, page 138)

Handful fresh coriander leaves, half
 reserved for garnish

1 Put the noodles in a large bowl and fill it with hot water to cover. When the noodles have softened, after about 15 minutes, drain, return to the bowl and set aside.

2 Heat a wok over a high heat. Add 2 tablespoons of the oil and swirl to coat the wok. When the oil is hot, add the onion, garlic and ginger and stir-fry for about 2 minutes until softened. Season with salt and pepper.

3 Combine the sambal with the eggs and stir to blend. Add the remaining 1 tablespoon oil to the wok, add the egg mixture and stir vigorously for about 1 minute until the eggs are just cooked through. Add the tempeh, lime juice and soy sauce and stir-fry for 1 minute. Add the noodles and red pepper and stir-fry for 1–2 minutes until heated through. Taste to adjust the seasoning. Add all but the reserved coriander and toss. Transfer to individual serving plates, garnish with the remaining coriander and serve.

Ming's tips:

For palatability and safety, be sure to heat the seitan thoroughly in the final step.

I've also had good luck using imitation chicken, a vegetable-based product, in this. Try using Quorn Chicken Style Pieces.

Video tip:

Watch the video to see my tutorial on imitation meats.

To Drink:

Ginger ale or iced green tea, sweetened with ginger syrup (page 184), and flavoured with lime juice to taste

The day I discovered black garlic I was overjoyed. Made from ordinary garlic that's fermented and dried, it tastes like a cross between roasted garlic and Chinese black beans. It would be difficult to find a more umami-rich ingredient – I use black garlic often in stir-fries and stews, where it kicks dishes into the stratosphere. Here, it does its thing for a simple courgette stir-fry that's brightened with fresh mint. The dish turns out to be a major wow.

COURGETTE – ONION STIR-FRY
with Black Garlic

SERVES 4

1 tablespoon rapeseed (canola) oil

2 large onions, cut into 1cm dice

Sea salt and freshly ground black pepper

6 black garlic cloves (see Tip), roughly chopped

1 tablespoon finely chopped fresh ginger

3 large courgettes, roll-cut into 2.5cm pieces (see Tip)

1 tablespoon naturally brewed soy sauce

480ml fresh vegetable stock or low-sodium bought

1 tablespoon cornflour mixed with 1 tablespoon water

10g mint leaves, torn

1–1.3kg cooked 50-50 White and Brown Rice (page 13)

1 Heat a wok over a high heat. Add the oil and swirl to coat the pan. When the oil is hot, add the onions and stir-fry for about 1 minute until soft. Season with salt and pepper. Add the black garlic and ginger and stir-fry for 1 minute.

2 Add the courgettes, season with salt and stir-fry for 2 minutes, then add the soy sauce and stock. Simmer for 3–4 minutes until the liquid is reduced by one-quarter. Whisk in half the cornflour mixture and simmer for about 1 minute until the mixture is glazed and lightly thickened. Adjust the seasoning with salt and pepper, if necessary. Add the mint, toss and serve with the rice.

Ming's tips:

Black garlic is available in heads or cloves, which come in airless bags. If you can't get black garlic, use 2 garlic cloves finely chopped with 1 tablespoon fermented black beans.

To roll-cut the courgettes and other vegetables, first slice away the stem ends on an angle. Roll the vegetable about a quarter turn away from you and slice again at the same angle about 2.5cm further down or the length your recipe suggests. Continue rolling and slicing until the vegetable has been entirely cut.

To Drink:

A Chardonnay, like Eric Chevalier, from the Loire Valley in France

This dish was inspired by the Singaporean hawker-style carrot cake *chai tow kway* and by my maternal grandfather's wonderful mooli pancakes, which also originated in Singapore. My version includes both vegetables for great texture and is characteristically fiery. You can serve these as a starter, but they're also good as a main dish with a salad.

SINGAPOREAN CARROT-MOOLI
Pancakes with Chilli Sauce

SERVES 4

3 tablespoons rapeseed (canola) oil, plus extra if needed

1 tablespoon finely chopped garlic

1 bunch spring onions, white and green parts, 1 tablespoon of the greens reserved for garnish

Sea salt and freshly ground black pepper

1 large mooli, peeled and grated

1 large carrot, peeled and grated

155g rice flour

5 large eggs, beaten

2 heaped teaspoons sambal

3 tablespoons ketjap manis

Juice of 1 lime

1 Heat a large heavy sauté pan or cast-iron frying pan over a medium-high heat. Add 1 tablespoon of the oil and swirl to coat the pan. When the oil is hot, add the garlic and all but the reserved spring onions and sauté, stirring, for about 30 seconds until fragrant. Season with salt and pepper. Add the mooli and carrot and sauté, stirring, for about 2 minutes until softened. Season with salt and transfer to a medium bowl to cool. Wipe out the pan.

2 Add the rice flour to a large bowl and whisk in the eggs to make a batter. Add 1 heaped teaspoon of the sambal and 1 tablespoon of the ketjap manis and whisk to blend. Add the cooled mixture and blend.

3 Line a large plate or platter with kitchen paper. Heat the pan over a medium-high heat. Add the remaining 2 tablespoons oil and swirl to coat the pan. When the oil is hot, ladle in enough of the batter to make 3 pancakes about 6cm in diameter. Use the bottom of the ladle or spatula to flatten the pancakes to size. Cook for 1–2 minutes until the undersides have browned. Using a large spatula, flip the pancakes and cook the second side for 2 minutes until browned. Transfer to the kitchen paper to drain. Repeat with the remaining batter, adding more oil if needed.

4 In a small bowl, combine the lime juice, the remaining 1 heaped teaspoon sambal and the remaining 2 tablespoons ketjap manis.

5 Transfer the pancakes to a large serving plate, drizzle with the sambal mixture, garnish with the reserved spring onion greens and serve immediately.

Ming's tip:
Make the vegetables and batter ahead of time, keep covered with cling film in the fridge for up to 24 hours and cook the pancakes when your guests show up.

To Drink:

A chilled Singapore beer, like Tiger, or Tsing Tao, from China

Years ago I had the best couscous of my life at Le Zerda Cafe in Paris. It was steamed over broth, which gave it great flavour and a light, fluffy texture. I've adopted this method for this great dish, which features a savoury ragout of aubergine, sweet potatoes, courgettes and red peppers. Diners add dollops of harissa mixed with yogurt to their servings, just the right hot-cooling finale. This is another great dinner party dish.

VEGGIE RAGOUT
with Couscous and Harissa Sauce

SERVES 4

280g traditional (not quick-cook) fine wholemeal couscous

Sea salt

2 tablespoons extra-virgin olive oil

1 large red onion, cut into 1cm dice

1 tablespoon finely chopped garlic

1 tablespoon finely chopped fresh ginger

1 tablespoon finely chopped fermented black beans

Freshly ground black pepper

1 large aubergine, diced

2 medium sweet potatoes, peeled and diced

2 large courgettes, cut into 1cm dice

2 large red peppers, diced

1–2 tablespoons naturally brewed soy sauce, to taste

2 x 400g cans chopped plum tomatoes

1 litre fresh vegetable stock or low-sodium bought

1 tablespoon harissa

245g fat-free natural Greek yogurt

1 Put the couscous in a large bowl. Cover with room-temperature water and allow the couscous to soak for 1 hour. Add a pinch of salt and rub it into the couscous, breaking up any lumps.

2 Meanwhile, heat a large saucepan over a medium-high heat. Add the oil and swirl to coat the base. When the oil is hot, add the onion, garlic, ginger and black beans and season with salt and pepper. Sauté, stirring, for 2–3 minutes until softened. Add the aubergine and sweet potatoes, season with salt and pepper and sauté, stirring, for about 4 minutes until softened. Add the courgettes and sauté, stirring, for about 2 minutes until tender. Season with salt and pepper. Add the red peppers, soy sauce to taste and tomatoes and stir. Add the stock, taste to adjust the seasoning with salt and pepper, if necessary, and bring to a simmer.

3 Line a colander or steamer basket that will fit into the pan with muslin and place the couscous in it. Fit the colander into the top of the pan and cover with foil, crimping it tightly around the pan edge to avoid steam escaping. Simmer for 45 minutes until the ragout and the couscous are cooked.

4 Meanwhile, in a small serving bowl, combine the harissa and yogurt. Season with salt. Mound the couscous in the centre of individual plates. Surround with the ragout, and spoon additional liquid from the ragout around it. Dollop the yogurt mixture on top and serve with the remaining mixture on the side.

To Drink:

A Chenin Blanc, like Mulderbosch

This dish is dedicated to my grandfather Yeh Yeh, who came from Hunan, where spicy dishes rule. He made his own sambal with chillies he grew in his Dayton, Ohio garden. As a kid I would try to outdo him in the how-hot-can-you-take-it eating department – let's just say that I did my very best. This great aubergine medley touches all the Hunanese flavour bases – it's savoury, sweet and tart as well as spicy and satisfies non-meat eaters and carnivores equally.

HUNAN GLAZED AUBERGINE
with Rice

SERVES 4 AS A SIDE DISH

3 tablespoons rice vinegar

6 tablespoons naturally brewed soy sauce

1 heaped tablespoon sambal

2 tablespoons maple syrup

80ml plus 1 tablespoon rapeseed (canola) oil, plus extra if needed

5 large or 6 medium Japanese aubergines, cut into 6cm spears (see Tip)

Sea salt and freshly ground black pepper

2 bunches spring onions, white and green parts, cut into 5mm-thick slices, 1½ tablespoons of the greens reserved for garnish

2 tablespoons finely chopped garlic

1 tablespoon finely chopped fresh ginger

1 teaspoon toasted sesame oil

1 teaspoon toasted sesame seeds

1–1.3kg cooked 50-50 White and Brown Rice (page 13)

1 In a small bowl, combine the vinegar, soy sauce, sambal and maple syrup. Stir well and set aside. Line a large plate with kitchen paper.

2 Heat a wok over a high heat. Add the 80ml oil and swirl to coat the pan. When the oil begins to smoke, add the aubergine and season with salt and pepper. Allow one side of the aubergine to brown, then turn and cook on the other side, 3–4 minutes in total, adding more oil if needed. With a slotted spoon, transfer the aubergine to the kitchen paper to drain.

3 Heat the wok over a high heat. Add the remaining 1 tablespoon oil and swirl to coat. When the oil is hot, add all but the reserved spring onions, the garlic and ginger and stir-fry for about 1 minute until fragrant. Add the vinegar mixture and simmer for 3–4 minutes until syrupy. Add the aubergine and toss, then add the sesame oil and a pinch of the sesame seeds and stir-fry for about 1 minute until the aubergine is glazed.

4 Spread the rice on a serving platter and top with the aubergine. Garnish with the reserved spring onion greens and remaining sesame seeds and serve.

Ming's tip:

To cut the aubergines into spears, trim and cut each lengthways into thirds. Cut each length into thirds again and then halve to make 6cm spears.

Video tip:

Watch the video to see me demonstrate my simple technique for preparing the aubergines.

To Drink:

An off-dry Gerwürtztraminer, like Trimbach

People think chow mein is an American invention, but it's a venerable Chinese noodle stir-fry. This version celebrates mushrooms – shiitakes, ordinary button and oyster – and also includes jicama for crunch. My mum would have made this with fresh water chestnuts, but they're laborious to prep. Jicama provides similar sweetness and crunch, and readying it is much easier on the cook. If all you've had is standard chicken chow mein, you must try this.

THREE-MUSHROOM AND JICAMA CHOW MEIN

SERVES 4

350g fresh or 225g dried egg
    noodles

Sea salt

2 tablespoons plus 1 teaspoon
    rapeseed (canola) oil

2 tablespoons finely chopped garlic

1 tablespoon finely chopped fresh
    ginger

1 bunch spring onions, white and
    green parts, 2 tablespoons of the
    greens reserved for garnish

Freshly ground black pepper

150g shiitake mushrooms, stems
    removed, cut into 5mm-thick slices

150g button mushrooms, stems
    removed, thinly sliced

150g oyster mushrooms, cored,
    halved if large and torn into pieces

1 large jicama, peeled and cut
    into thin strips

1 red pepper, diced

240ml fresh vegetable stock or low-
    sodium bought

4 tablespoons vegetarian oyster sauce

1 teaspoon toasted sesame oil

To Drink:

A Californian Pinot Noir

1 Fill a large bowl with water and add ice. Separate the noodles by hand. In a wok, cook the noodles in abundant boiling salted water for 3–4 minutes until al dente if fresh, or 8–10 minutes if dried. Transfer the noodles to the iced water. When cold, drain well, transfer to a plate and set aside.

2 Heat the wok over a high heat. Add the oil and swirl to coat the pan. When the oil is hot, add the garlic, ginger and all but the reserved spring onions and stir-fry for about 1 minute until fragrant. Season with salt and black pepper. Add the shiitakes and stir-fry for 2 minutes. Add the 1 teaspoon oil and the button and oyster mushrooms, season with salt and pepper and stir-fry for about 1 minute until all the mushrooms are soft. Add the jicama and red pepper and stir-fry for 30 seconds, then add the stock and oyster sauce. Bring to a simmer, add the noodles, toss and heat through for about 2 minutes.

3 Transfer the chow mein to a serving platter or large pasta bowl. Drizzle with the sesame oil, garnish with the reserved spring onion greens and serve.

Ming's tips:

It's easiest to use a salad spinner for prepping the noodles. Fill its bowl with water and add ice. Drain the cooked noodles in the spinner and return it to the bowl. When the noodles are cold, drain the noodles and spin them dry.

To toss vulnerable ingredients like cooked noodles in a wok or another pan, it's best to flip them. Practise flipping using a frying pan and rice or beans outdoors. It doesn't take long to get the knack.

You've probably enjoyed the more traditional version of this dish. It always contains curry and rice noodles, and can also include red-roasted pork, prawns and eggs. It is, interestingly, unknown in Singapore, but undoubtedly takes its name from the profusion of Indian restaurants there, which of course serve curries. My version features smoked tofu and crisp beansprouts, and is every bit as satisfying as meat and seafood curries.

SINGAPORE CURRY TOFU NOODLES

SERVES 4

200g rice vermicelli or bean thread noodles

2½ tablespoons rapeseed (canola) oil

1 tablespoon finely chopped garlic

1 tablespoon finely chopped fresh ginger

1 red or green jalapeño chilli, finely chopped

2 tablespoons curry powder, preferably Madras

1 large onion, cut into 5mm-thick slices

Sea salt and freshly ground black pepper

3 large eggs, beaten

1 red pepper, cut into 5mm-wide strips (see Tip, page 138)

2 x 225g packs smoked tofu, or one 400g package firm tofu, cut widthways into 5mm-thick slices

225g beansprouts, ends trimmed, washed and spun dry

1 tablespoon rice vinegar

To Drink:

A Riesling or a lager, like Foster's

1 Put the noodles in a large bowl and fill it with hot water to cover. When the noodles have softened, after about 15 minutes for rice vermicelli or 10 minutes for bean threads, drain and set aside.

2 Add 1 tablespoon oil to the wok, swirl to coat the pan and heat over a high heat. Add the garlic, ginger and jalapeño and stir-fry for about 30 seconds until aromatic. Add the curry powder and onion and stir-fry for about 1 minute until softened. Add another ½ tablespoon oil and season with salt and pepper. Push the onion mixture to one side of the wok and add the remaining 1 tablespoon oil to the other side. When the oil is hot, add the eggs, season with a touch of salt and cook, stirring, for about 1 minute until scrambled.

3 Combine the eggs with the onion mixture. Add the red pepper, tofu and noodles and heat through, tossing, for 1–2 minutes. Add the beansprouts and vinegar, season with salt and pepper and heat through, tossing, for 1–2 minutes. Transfer to a platter or large bowl and serve.

This dish has a mixed pedigree. It's based partly on eight treasure rice, a traditional Chinese pudding whose treasures include lotus seeds, dates and red beans. Its other forbear is *jong zi*, a delicious dim sum made with glutinous rice and pork. I've taken the idea of a savoury yet meatless rice dish filled with good things and run with it, creating a great fried rice that's truly a meal in one. This is another dish that meat-lovers as well as the meat-averse will devour.

EIGHT TREASURE FRIED RICE

SERVES 4

5 tablespoons rapeseed (canola) oil
4 large eggs, beaten
Sea salt
1 tablespoon finely chopped garlic
1 tablespoon finely chopped fresh ginger
1 serrano chilli, finely chopped
1 large courgette, diced
1 bunch spring onions, white and green parts, thinly sliced, 1 tablespoon of the greens reserved for garnish
Freshly ground black pepper
150g shiitake mushrooms, stems removed, cut into 3mm-thick slices
2 tablespoons wheat-free tamari
150g shelled edamame
1.2kg 50-50 White and Brown Rice, cooked and cooled (page 13)
2 tablespoons toasted sesame seeds

1 Line a large plate with kitchen paper. Heat a wok over a high heat. Add 4 tablespoons of the oil and swirl to coat. When the oil is hot, add the eggs and season with salt. When the eggs puff, stir vigorously, then transfer the eggs to the kitchen paper to drain.

2 Add the remaining 1 tablespoon oil to the wok, swirl to coat and heat over a high heat. When the oil is hot, add the garlic, ginger and chilli and stir-fry for about 30 seconds until aromatic. Lower the heat to medium-high, add the courgette and all but the reserved spring onions and stir-fry for about 1 minute until slightly softened. Season with salt and pepper. Add the shiitakes and tamari and stir-fry for about 2 minutes until soft. Add the edamame and the eggs. Stir to break up the eggs, then add the rice. Stir for about 2 minutes until heated through. Adjust the seasoning with salt and pepper. Transfer to a large serving platter, garnish with the reserved spring onion greens and the sesame seeds and serve.

To Drink:

A Chardonnay, like Cameron Hughes Lot 220

I love tofu because, like a blank canvas, it invites invention. Here, it's shallow-fried and then glazed with a garlic, chilli and peanut mixture, so it's not only good for you but totally delicious. I like to use raw peanuts for this, which are then toasted, but feel free to buy roasted unsalted peanuts and omit the toasting step.

CRISPY TOFU
with Peanut–Garlic Glaze

SERVES 4

75g raw peanuts (see headnote)
2 garlic cloves, peeled
1 bird's eye or serrano chilli, stem
　removed, thinly sliced
Sea salt and freshly ground
　black pepper
Juice of 1 lime
4 tablespoons ketjap manis, or
　2 tablespoons black treacle
155g rice flour
2 tablespoons cornflour
2 x 350g packs silken tofu, cut
　lengthways into 1cm-thick slices
Rapeseed (canola) oil for frying
2 tablespoons thinly sliced chives,
　plus extra whole chives for garnish

1 Put the peanuts in a medium sauté pan and toast over a medium heat, stirring frequently, for 2 minutes. Lower the heat and toast for 1–2 minutes until golden.

2 Using a mortar and pestle, or in a mini food processor, grind together or process the garlic, chilli and a pinch of salt until smooth. Add the peanuts and grind or process just until the nuts are chopped. If using a mortar and pestle, you may have to grind them in batches. Add the lime juice and ketjap manis and stir or pulse to blend. Add a pinch of salt and set aside.

3 On a large flat plate, mix together the rice flour and cornflour. Season the tofu with salt and pepper and dredge on both sides in the flour mixture.

4 Line a large plate with kitchen paper. Fill a large straight-sided sauté pan with 2.5cm of oil. Heat over medium heat to 180°C on a deep-frying thermometer. Working in 2 batches, if necessary, add the tofu and fry, turning once, for about 6 minutes until golden. Transfer to the kitchen paper and then sprinkle with a pinch of salt.

5 Place a few of the whole chives on individual serving plates. Top with the tofu, spoon the glaze over it, sprinkle with the sliced chives and serve.

Video tip:
Watch the video to see my tutorial on tofu.

To Drink:
A Champagne or sparkling wine,
like Marquis de la Tour Brut

CHAPTER 7

Sweets

When the dessert's homemade, the meal is special. If you're reluctant to make sweets, don't be. The desserts here are as approachable as they are delicious, and bring something new to your table.

Five-Spice Tarte Tatin, for example, takes the traditional dessert of caramelised apples on a buttery crust eastwards. Similarly, Lemongrass Panna Cotta's heavenly texture seems even lighter due to its Thai flavouring. And Cardamom Chocolate Cake, a fudgy bittersweet treat, is enhanced by cardamom's warm, spicy–sweet taste.

As a kid my favourite dessert was a hot fudge sundae. The combination of cold ice cream and hot sauce did it for me. Chocolate Banana Bread Sundaes up the ante on that great treat by adding sliced coconut-flavoured banana bread. The recipe also yields a second loaf, which you can use for more sundaes or enjoy on its own.

I was never a cookie freak until I devised Almond Oatmeal Cookies. Their chewy goodness gives chocolate chip cookies a run for their money. Definitely not homey, Mango Rum Granita makes an elegant dessert, but is ridiculously easy to do. It's another sweet that both new and veteran cooks will love.

I first had tarte tatin when working as a sous-chef at restaurant Natasha, in Paris. I watched, fascinated, as its chef, Jean-Marc Forteneau, prepared it. He caramelised apples in a frying pan, then topped them with pastry. When he inverted the tart onto a plate and the luscious apples were revealed resting *on* the crust, I couldn't have been happier. Until I tasted the tart, which was amazing. My version is all you want from a tarte tatin plus it's flavoured with five-spice powder, which takes the usual cinnamon–apple combo to a higher, more interesting place. Served warm with vanilla ice cream, this is as good as it gets. No, better.

FIVE-SPICE TARTE TATIN

SERVES 8

CRUST

3 large egg yolks
315g plain flour
2 tablespoons caster sugar
225g unsalted butter, cold, diced

6 Granny Smith apples, peeled,
 cored and quartered
300g granulated sugar
Juice of 1 lemon
2 teaspoons five-spice powder
55g unsalted butter

To Drink:

A Prosecco, like Lunetta,
or a Calvados

1 First make the crust. In a small bowl, combine the egg yolks with 60ml very cold water. In a food processor, combine the flour and caster sugar. Add the butter and pulse for about 10 seconds until the mixture resembles coarse meal. With the processor running, add the egg yolk mixture in a slow, steady stream and process just until the dough holds together and is no longer crumbly. Transfer the dough to a work surface and divide it in half. Make a ball of each half and flatten into discs. Wrap each disc separately in cling film and refrigerate for 1 hour or up to a week. If not using the second dough within that time, wrap it in cling film and then in foil, tuck into a resealable plastic bag and freeze for up to 3 months for another use.

2 In a large bowl, combine the apples, 100g of the granulated sugar, the lemon juice and five-spice powder. Toss and leave to stand for 30 minutes. Drain the apples, reserving 2 tablespoons of the juice.

3 Preheat the oven to 200°C/fan 180°C/Gas Mark 6. Melt the butter in a 25cm cast-iron frying pan over a medium-low heat. Add the remaining sugar and the reserved apple juice and cook, stirring constantly, for 15–20 minutes until a light caramel brown syrup forms.

4 Working from the outside in, lay the apple quarters over the base of the pan. Slide one apple quarter to the side and baste the apples, while keeping a watchful eye, and cook for about 3 minutes until the caramel is dark amber. Cook for about a further 10 minutes until the apples are al dente.

5 Place one of the dough discs on a large sheet of baking paper and roll it out into a round about 5mm thick that will fit the pan with about a 5mm overhang. Top the apples with the dough, tucking the edges of the dough between the apples and the side of the pan. Bake for 10 minutes, rotate the pan and bake for about a further 10 minutes until the crust is brown.

6 Remove the tart from the oven and leave to rest for 20 minutes. Run a knife around the inside edge of the pan to loosen the tart. Top with a serving dish and, being careful of the hot caramel, invert the pan and dish. The tart should drop onto the plate easily; if it doesn't, reinvert the pan and place it on the hob over a medium-high heat for 1–2 minutes to melt the caramel further and help the tart to release. Cut into slices and serve hot, warm or at room temperature.

Ming's tip:

This recipe makes enough dough for 2 tarts. Use one half and store the other, as the recipe instructs, for another tart or quiche.

This is my version of a cake created by Damien 'Big D' D'Silva, a linebacker of a chef, who appeared on *Simply Ming*. His cake featured pearl tapioca, whose wonderful texture I love. The pearls are clearly visible in both of our versions, suspended in a cooked egg mixture. I've upped the ante, though, by flavouring the cake with coconut and lime and serving it with papaya. This makes a unique dessert, one I urge you to try.

TAPIOCA COCONUT CAKE

SERVES 10

15–25g unsalted butter,
   for greasing the tin
1–2 tablespoons demerara sugar

PUDDING

175g small pearl tapioca
480ml whole milk
150g dark brown sugar
2 x 400ml cans unsweetened coconut
   milk
Pinch of sea salt
Juice and zest of 1 lime
3 large eggs
3 large egg yolks

PAPAYA

1 papaya, peeled, deseeded and diced
Juice and zest of 1 lime

To Drink:

A lychee tea

1 Cut a piece of baking paper to fit the base of a 23cm springform cake tin (see Tip). Grease the base and the sides of the tin with the butter. Place the baking paper in the tin and grease with butter. Add the demerara sugar and tilt the tin to coat the sides evenly.

2 Make the pudding. Put the tapioca in a medium bowl and add cold water to cover it. Leave the tapioca to soak for 1 hour. Drain the tapioca in a large sieve, rinse well under tepid running water and set aside in the sieve.

3 In a large saucepan, combine the milk, brown sugar, coconut milk and salt and bring to a simmer over a medium heat. Add the tapioca, stir, lower the heat to medium-low and simmer, stirring, for 1–2 minutes until the tapioca is translucent but still slightly raw at the centre. Pour the pudding into a medium-sized baking tray, add the lime juice and zest and stir to combine. Leave to cool for 5 minutes, stirring occasionally, then transfer to a large bowl.

4 Preheat the oven to 180°C/fan 160°C/Gas Mark 4. In a medium bowl, combine the eggs and yolks and whisk until just blended. Pour the eggs over the tapioca, fold to combine and pour into the prepared tin. Bake for 35–40 minutes until the cake is golden brown in spots and still jiggly in the centre. Transfer to a rack to cool, then refrigerate in the pan for at least 8 hours or overnight.

5 In a medium bowl, combine the papaya and lime juice and zest. Remove the tin side, place a serving plate on the cake and invert. Remove the tin base, peel off the paper, cut the cake into wedges and serve with the papaya.

Ming's tips:

To cut baking paper for lining the baking tin, put the tin base on a sheet of the paper. With a pen or pencil, draw around the base, then cut out the circle about 3mm in from the line.

After baking, the cake will seem unset, but will become firm when refrigerated.

Panna cotta, that silky, eggless Italian custard, presents a challenge. You need to have enough gelatine in it so that it holds its shape, but not so much that the dessert becomes bouncy. This version achieves just the right ethereal texture – and gives an impression of particular lightness due to the refreshing lemongrass. The panna cotta is topped with sliced strawberries, a final elegant touch.

LEMONGRASS PANNA COTTA

SERVES 8

4 lemongrass stalks, white parts only, pounded and cut into 1cm-thick pieces (see Tip)

480ml double cream, plus extra as needed

720ml whole milk

7 tablespoons granulated sugar

1 vanilla pod, split lengthways

2½ teaspoons granulated unflavoured gelatine

450g strawberries, washed, hulled and sliced 5mm thick

Juice and zest of 1 lemon

1 A day in advance, fill a large bowl with water and add ice. In a large saucepan, combine the lemongrass, 480ml cream, the milk and 6 tablespoons of the sugar. Scrape the seeds from the vanilla pod and add to the mixture. Tie the vanilla pod in a loose knot and add that too. Bring all to a simmer over a medium heat. Simmer gently, stirring occasionally, for about 5 minutes. Transfer the pan to the water bath. When the mixture has cooled to room temperature, refrigerate overnight in the pan to steep.

2 Combine the gelatine with 80ml room-temperature water in a small non-reactive bowl. Whisk over a small saucepan of simmering water for about 1 minute until the gelatine completely dissolves.

3 Meanwhile, strain the lemongrass mixture into a 1-litre measuring jug, pressing to extract as much liquid as possible. Add additional cream through the sieve to measure 960ml and return the mixture to the saucepan. Bring the cream to a simmer over a medium heat. Add 120ml of the cream to the gelatine to temper, stir, return the gelatin mixture to the cream and gently stir to combine. Pour the mixture slowly through a sieve (to break up any bubbles), dividing it between 8 × 125ml ramekins. Refrigerate for 8 hours or overnight until set.

4 In a medium bowl, combine the strawberries, lemon juice and zest and the remaining 1 tablespoon sugar. Stir and leave to stand for 15 minutes.

5 To serve, place the ramekins on dessert plates. Top with the strawberries or serve them on the side.

Ming's tip:

Pound the lemongrass stalks with a meat mallet, the side of a big knife or a small heavy pan. Remove the fibrous inner core at the end of the lemongrass. Cut the stalks lengthways to break them up further, then cut crossways into pieces as the recipe instructs.

To Drink:

A Moscato d'Asti, like Michele Chiaro Nivole

Here's a sophisticated dessert that's a cinch to make. A granita that's made in the freezer –
no special equipment is needed – it also features one of my favourite fruits, mango, and a touch
of rum, or vanilla if you're serving this to kids or teetotalers. No mangoes? Then by all means
use pineapple, or any juicy fruit. (Bananas, for example, won't do.) Light and refreshing, this makes
a particularly good finish to a rich meal.

MANGO RUM GRANITA

SERVES 4

2 ripe mangoes, peeled, stoned
  and roughly chopped
6 tablespoons dark rum,
  preferably Gosling's, or
  1 teaspoon vanilla extract
120ml soda water or sparkling
  water
Juice and zest of 2 oranges
Juice of 1 lime
2 tablespoons runny honey, plus
  extra if needed
Pinch of sea salt

1 A day in advance, in a food processor or blender, combine the mangoes,
4 tablespoons of the rum, the soda water, orange and lime juices and 1 tablespoon
of the honey, and process until smooth. Taste, and if not sweet enough, add
more honey. Add the salt.

2 Transfer to a 20cm-square glass or metal container – the mixture should make a
layer that is 2.5–4cm thick – and freeze overnight.

3 In a small bowl, combine the remaining 2 tablespoons rum, the orange zest
and the remaining 1 tablespoon honey and stir. Cover and set aside while the granita
freezes. Chill 4 martini glasses in the freezer.

4 Before serving, using the back of a fork, scrape the frozen granita into the martini
glasses. Place a spoonful of the zest mixture in the centre of each and serve.

Ming's tips:

To select a ripe mango, first sniff the fruit – it should be fragrant. Press it gently;
your finger should make an indentation that 'bounces back'.

If you do omit the rum, the granita will freeze solid. Leave it to stand for
10 minutes at room temperature so that you'll then be able to scrape the
granita into serving glasses.

Video tip:

Watch the video to learn my simple technique for preparing mango.

To Drink:
The dark rum you use for
the granita

If you haven't tried pots de crème, the classic French custard, you must. Its velvety smoothness takes custard about as far as it can go. This version is flavoured with coffee, a drink I'm fully behind. I advise you to get maitake coffee to flavour these – it contains maitake mushroom powder, which sounds strange but isn't; the powder lends no flavour of its own but reduces the coffee's acidity, so the drink is sweeter. Whatever coffee you use, this is a wonderful dessert.

COFFEE POTS DE CRÈME

SERVES 6

480ml whole milk
150g caster sugar
20g ground coffee, preferably
   Maitake (see Tip)
1 vanilla pod, split lengthways
240ml double cream
7 large egg yolks

1 Line a fine-mesh sieve with muslin. In a large saucepan, combine the milk, half the sugar and the coffee. Scrape the seeds from the vanilla pod into the mixture and add the pod. Bring to a simmer over a medium-high heat – about 3 minutes. Pour through the sieve into a medium bowl and add the cream.

2 Preheat the oven to 150°C/fan 130°C/Gas Mark 2. In a large bowl, combine the egg yolks with the remaining sugar and whisk vigorously to dissolve the sugar. Gradually add 240ml of the hot cream mixture while whisking vigorously, to temper the yolks. Add the remaining cream in a steady stream. Whisk to combine.

3 Arrange 6 × 125ml ramekins in a roasting tin. Divide the cream mixture between the ramekins and add enough hot water to the tin to come halfway up the side of the ramekins. Bake for about 45 minutes until set but an area in the centre about the size of a 5p coin still quivers. Leave the ramekins in the water bath on the work surface for 15 minutes to cool slightly before removing. Cool for 30 minutes, then chill in the fridge for at least 8 hours or overnight and serve.

Ming's tips:

The pots de crème have a hint-of-coffee taste. For a more pronounced flavour, allow the sweetened coffee mixture to steep for 20 minutes before straining it.

You can use small (about 125ml) coffee cups in place of the ramekins. If you do, allow the cooked pots de crème to sit in their water bath for 20 minutes before removing and chilling them.

If you don't have Maitake Coffee on hand, use your favourite medium roast coffee.

To Drink:
Ming Tsai's Maitake Coffee

Chocolate chip cookies, back off! These chewy-gooey almond cookies are the best cookie ever, full stop. I ate at least 16 of them on the day we shot the photos for this book, and I'm not usually a cookie lover. The deep sweetness of the brown sugar and the agave syrup, plus the richness of the almonds from the almond flour, make these irresistible. These are the cookies for which a cold milk accompaniment was invented.

ALMOND OATMEAL COOKIES

MAKES 24

80g porridge oats
140g almond flour
125g plain flour
½ teaspoon sea salt
115g unsalted butter
150g dark brown sugar
2 tablespoons light agave syrup
   or runny honey
1 teaspoon bicarbonate of soda

1 Place 2 shelves in the bottom and middle positions of the oven. Preheat the oven to 180°C/fan 160°C/Gas Mark 4. In a large bowl, combine the oats, flours and salt and set aside. Fill a tea kettle or small saucepan with about 250ml water and bring to the boil.

2 In a medium saucepan, melt the butter over a medium heat. Add the brown sugar and syrup and stir, then add 2 tablespoons of the boiling water. Bring just to the boil, add the bicarbonate of soda and whisk to blend. As soon as the mixture bubbles, remove the pan from the heat and continue to whisk until the bubbles subside. Whisk for about 1 minute to incorporate air, then pour over the flour mixture. Using a rubber spatula, fold the liquid ingredients into the dry ingredients to make a dough.

3 Roll the dough into balls slightly smaller than golf balls. Place 5cm apart on 2 baking sheets and press down to flatten. Bake for 7–8 minutes until lightly browned all over. Don't overbake; the cookies should be chewy in the centre. Transfer the cookies to a wire rack and leave to cool.

Ming's tip:

You can make awesome ice cream sandwiches with these cookies (as pictured). Let the cookies cool completely. Place a generous scoop of the flavour-of-your-choice ice cream, or a non-dairy equivalent, on the flat side of one cookie. Sandwich with a second one, pressing down to flatten the ice cream into a disc shape. Roll the sides in toasted flaked almonds for extra crunch. Enjoy immediately or wrap them individually in cling film and store in the freezer for a quick treat.

To Drink:
Cold milk or a nondairy drink
rice milk.

This recipe doubles your pleasure. You make exotically flavoured coconut and lime banana bread, which is sliced and used in sundaes that also include, besides your favourite ice cream, luscious chocolate ganache. The recipe yields two loaves – enough to make sundaes for a big party – but you can use one loaf only and half the ganache for a smaller event, and store the other loaf and the remaining ganache for a later day. It's great to have banana bread on hand; I like to let it get stale, slice it, then brown it in butter, or just nibble it as is. These sundaes end any meal with a major bang.

CHOCOLATE BANANA BREAD SUNDAES

MAKES 2 LOAVES; SERVES 16

375g plain flour
2 teaspoons bicarbonate of soda
½ teaspoon sea salt
225g unsalted butter, at room
   temperature
300g caster sugar
5 large eggs
85g sweetened dried flaked
   coconut, toasted (see Tip),
   plus 45g for decorating
4 very ripe bananas, mashed
2 teaspoons vanilla extract
Zest of 1 lime

GANACHE
225g dark chocolate chips
15g unsalted butter
360ml double cream
1 tablespoon caster sugar

Ice cream for serving

1 Preheat the oven to 180°C/fan 160°C/Gas Mark 4 and place a rack in the centre. Spray two 13 x 23cm loaf tins well with non-stick cooking spray. Sift the flour, bicarbonate of soda and salt into a medium bowl and set aside.

2 In the bowl of an electric mixer, combine the butter and sugar and beat on a low speed for 30 seconds to combine. Increase the speed to high and beat for 1–2 minutes until smooth. Reduce the speed to medium and add the eggs one at a time, scraping the bowl between additions. Add the 95g coconut, the bananas, vanilla extract and lime zest, and mix just until incorporated. Reduce the speed to low, add the flour mixture gradually and beat to combine.

3 Divide the mixture evenly between the prepared tins and bake for 45–55 minutes until a skewer inserted in the middle comes out clean. Leave to rest for 10 minutes, then transfer to a wire rack to cool just until warm.

4 Meanwhile, make the ganache. Put the chocolate chips and butter in a medium heatproof bowl. In a medium saucepan, heat the cream over a medium heat until it simmers, then whisk in the sugar. When the sugar has dissolved, pour the mixture over the chocolate and butter and leave to stand for 2 minutes to melt the chocolate, then stir with a spatula to incorporate the chocolate into the cream.

5 Cut the loaves into 1cm-thick slices and halve each slice on the bias. Place a small scoop of ice cream in the bottom of each sundae bowl, sprinkle with some coconut and drizzle with the ganache. Place one half of a banana bread slice against one side of each of the bowls. Add a second scoop of ice cream and place a second banana bread half on the opposite side of the bowl. Drizzle with additional ganache, sprinkle with more coconut and serve immediately.

To Drink:
A dark rum, like Gosling's

Ming's tips:

Test the banana bread loaves frequently, as they go from gooiness at the centre to done very quickly.

You can buy toasted coconut, but to make it yourself, preheat the oven to 180°C/fan 160°C/Gas Mark 4. Line a baking sheet with baking paper. Spread sweetened dried flaked coconut on the sheet in a thin layer and toast, stirring every few minutes and watching carefully, for about 8 minutes until golden.

Refrigerate unused ganache in a glass container with a cover. Warm the ganache in the container in a hot water bath for about 10 minutes, or in the microwave, stirring it with a rubber spatula top to bottom, every 20 seconds for 2–3 minutes.

One of our signature Blue Ginger desserts consists of dark chocolate cake accompanied by cardamom-flavoured ice cream. Hmmm, I thought, why not add the wonderful cardamom flavour to the cake itself? Thought to dish, and here it is – a fudgy chocolate cake spiced with cardamom. This makes a sophisticated ending to any meal.

CARDAMOM CHOCOLATE CAKE

SERVES 12

125g plain chocolate chips
175g dark chocolate with over 50% cocoa solids, finely chopped
225g unsalted butter, diced
150g plus 70g granulated sugar
⅛ teaspoon sea salt
6 large eggs
1 tablespoon ground cardamom
110g icing sugar mixed with 1 teaspoon ground cardamom for decorating

1 Preheat the oven to 160°C/fan 140°C/Gas Mark 3 and place an oven shelf in the middle position. Spray a 20cm round cake tin with non-stick cooking spray.

2 Fill a medium saucepan half-full of water and place over a medium heat. In a medium heatproof bowl, combine the chocolates and butter and set aside.

3 In a small saucepan, combine the 150g granulated sugar with 120ml water and the salt and heat over a medium heat for 2–3 minutes just until the sugar has dissolved and the mixture just reaches a simmer. Pour the sugar mixture over the chocolates and butter and place over the saucepan to melt the chocolate. Stir the chocolate with a rubber spatula to melt it completely.

4 Meanwhile, in a large bowl, lightly beat the eggs. In a small bowl, combine the remaining granulated sugar and the cardamom. Gradually whisk the sugar mixture into the eggs and continue whisking to combine well. Drizzle about 120ml of the chocolate mixture into the egg mixture, stirring, to temper. Fold in the remaining egg mixture until homogenous. Pour the mixture into the prepared tin, place in a larger baking dish and set on the oven shelf. Pour enough hot water into the larger pan to come halfway up the sides of the cake tin. Bake for 50–55 minutes until a skewer inserted in the middle comes out clean.

5 Transfer the cake in the tin to a wire rack to cool for about 30 minutes. Place a serving plate over the tin and invert to unmould. If the cake doesn't unmould, place a serving plate over the tin, invert, tape the tin a few times to loosen the cake, and unmould.

6 Using a fine-mesh sieve, sprinkle an even layer of the icing sugar mixture on the top of the cake and serve.

To Drink:
A Banyuls, like Les Clos de Paulilles, or another dessert wine

Video tip:
Watch the video to learn my foolproof technique for making this cake.

CHAPTER 8

Cocktails

I'm really excited to include cocktail recipes in a cookbook. It's a first, and there's a reason for it. Over the years Blue Ginger cocktails have earned a following. I'm often asked how we make drinks like Pineapple–Thai Basil Champagne Cocktail, Sake Cucumber Martini and Passion Fruit Mai Thai. Until now, only we had the recipes. Now you do too.

To ensure the best cocktails, I offer these tips:

- Whether used for shaking or in drinks, I always buy ice, and advise you to do the same. Bought cubes are uniform, crystal clear and convenient. Buy the biggest cubes you can find and make sure to keep the ice 'dry' by transferring it to a cooler before you make your drinks.

- Chill martini glasses in the freezer, or add iced water to them, swoosh it around and pour it out. Martinis really need to be glacier-cold. Thin shards of ice on the drink indicate that they're at the proper temperature.

- Shaking is key. Shake drinks for about 20 seconds until the outside of the shaker is very cold and beaded with sweat. You can make up to two drinks in a shaker at a time, but no more.

- Syrups used for drinks are made in quantity and can, and should, be stored for later use – please see the recipes.

I can't think of a better preface to a meal than a kir royale. So, being me, I wanted to create my own version. This is it – a wonderful combination of Champagne, pineapple and basil. Though Champagne is first choice, you can use a good bottle of any sparkling wine and you'll still have a great drink.

PINEAPPLE-THAI BASIL CHAMPAGNE COCKTAIL

SERVES 1

PINEAPPLE-THAI BASIL SYRUP

200g demerara sugar
310g fresh pineapple flesh, diced
4 large Thai basil sprigs,
   plus 1 for garnish

FOR EACH DRINK

175ml chilled dry Champagne
1 tablespoon Pineapple-Thai Basil
   syrup

1 Overnight or up to 24 hours in advance, make the syrup. In a medium saucepan, combine the sugar, pineapple and 240ml water. Bring to a simmer over a medium heat and simmer for about 20 minutes until the sugar is dissolved and the pineapple is soft. Remove from the heat and leave to cool for 2–3 minutes.

2 Very gently crush the basil leaves, but not the stems, in your hands. Add to the syrup, remove the pan from the heat and leave to cool to room temperature – about 30 minutes. Use the syrup immediately or store in the fridge in an airtight container for later use.

3 To make the cocktail, spoon 1 tablespoon of the syrup with a handful of pieces of pineapple into a Champagne flute. Slowly pour the Champagne into the flute, garnish with a fresh basil sprig and serve.

Ming's tips:

The syrup recipe makes about 720ml, enough for 24 drinks. Keep refrigerated in an airtight container for up to 2 weeks. The leftover syrup can be combined with sparkling water or club soda for a non-alcoholic drink, or use the syrup as a garnish for grilled chicken breasts with a squeeze of lime.

Feel free to use a less expensive sparkling wine in this recipe as well.

Video tip:

Watch the video to learn my simple technique for preparing the pineapple.

We created this terrific martini for Blue Ginger's opening. I've always been a great sake fan, and it seemed only natural to make a martini featuring it, in this case TY KU Sake Black. The cucumber adds tantalising flavour and texture – as you raise the glass to your lips, you smell it before you taste it, and the fragrance invites you to enjoy the drink.

SAKE CUCUMBER MARTINI

SERVES 1

90ml sake
50ml vodka
10cm length cucumber,
    peeled and julienned (see Tip)

1 Fill the tumbler of a Boston shaker with ice. Add the sake and vodka and shake for about 20 seconds until the ice has broken up.

2 Strain into a chilled martini glass. Add 4 or 5 pieces of the julienned cucumber and serve.

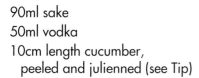

Ming's tip:

To julienne the cucumber, if there's a rounded end, square it off. Stand the cucumber on one end and cut it into even slices about 5mm thick. Stack the slices and cut into 5mm-wide strips.

MING.COM/INYOURKITCHEN/
RECIPE75

The inspiration for this drink was *tom kha gai*, the fiery Thai chicken soup with coconut. The 'translation', dish to drink, works beautifully – the vodka-based martini features cream of coconut, lime and tongue-tingling chilli. I love the drink's spiciness; it really opens the palate for the meal to come.

SPICY THAI COCONUT MARTINI

SERVES 1

CORIANDER- AND CHILLI-INFUSED VODKA

1 x 750ml bottle premium vodka
1 large bunch coriander, washed
2 tablespoons gochugaru (Korean chilli flakes)

FOR EACH DRINK

2 tablespoons demerara sugar
½1 teaspoon togarashi, or to taste
1 lime wedge
1 generous tablespoon cream of coconut
7.5ml Rose's lime juice
90ml coriander and chilli-infused vodka

1 First make the infused vodka. In a tall glass container with a snap-on lid, combine the vodka, coriander and gochugaru and leave to stand for 1 hour. Put a funnel into the empty vodka bottle and, using a fine-mesh sieve, strain the mixture back into the vodka bottle through the funnel.

2 On a small plate, combine the sugar and togarashi. Fill a martini glass with iced water to chill. When the glass is cold, discard the water. Rub the lime wedge around the glass rim, then dip the rim into the togarashi mixture to coat it.

3 Fill the tumbler of a Boston shaker with ice. Add the cream of coconut, Rose's and infused vodka, and shake for about 20 seconds until the ice has broken up. Strain into the glass, garnish with a coriander leaf taken from the infused vodka and serve.

Ming's tip:
The coriander and chilli-infused vodka makes about 720ml, enough for 8 drinks.

MING.COM/INYOURKITCHEN/RECIPE76

I call this a superfruit cooler. Superfruits, like melon and blueberry, are great for you, and are included in TY KU Liqueur and the flavoured vodka, both used here. Most important, though, is taste – and in that department, this cocktail excels, due to the liqueur and blueberry vodka, a great marriage. Try this on a hot summer day – or anytime.

SPARKLING BLUEBERRY COCKTAIL

SERVES 1

GINGER SYRUP

400g granulated sugar
about 2 large hands fresh ginger,
    peeled and cut into 3mm-thick slices

GIMLET MIX

350ml sweet and sour mix
125ml freshly squeezed lime juice
50ml ginger syrup

FOR EACH DRINK

40ml TY KU Liqueur
1 tablespoon blueberry vodka
1 teaspoon gimlet mix
1 teaspoon pomegranate purée
    or syrup
Soda water
1 very thin lime wheel

Ming's tip:

You will have plenty of leftover syrup. Use it to make your own ginger ale by combining it to taste with soda water, ice and a squeeze of lime juice. It's also great for sweetening tea.

1 First make the ginger syrup. In a medium saucepan, combine the sugar, 480ml water and ginger and bring to the boil over a high heat. Lower the heat and simmer for 40–45 minutes until the mixture is reduced by half. Strain and set aside.

2 For the gimlet mix, in a Mason jar or other container with a tight-fitting lid, combine the sweet and sour mix, lime juice and ginger syrup. Stir and refrigerate.

3 Fill the tumbler of a Boston shaker with ice. Add the TY KU liqueur, vodka, gimlet mix and pomegranate purée. Shake until the shaker is beaded with sweat and very cold to the touch. Taste and adjust any of the ingredients as needed. Pour the liquer mixture into a highball glass and top with a splash of the soda water. Garnish with the lime wheel and serve.

MING.COM/INYOURKITCHEN/
RECIPE77

As you can tell, I'm a huge Thai basil fan. I also love mojitos, the Cuban cocktail made with rum, lime juice and sparkling water. A mojito made with a Thai basil base is an instant East–West classic and a guaranteed crowd pleaser.

THAI BASIL MOJITO

SERVES 1

THAI BASIL SYRUP

400g demerara sugar
2 bunches Thai basil

FOR EACH DRINK

4 lime wedges
4 Thai basil leaves
Pinch of demerara sugar, plus extra
    for rimming the glass
2 tablespoons Thai basil syrup
40ml white rum
Soda water
Thai basil sprig

1 A day in advance, make the Thai basil syrup. In a medium saucepan, combine the sugar and 480ml water. Bring to a simmer over a medium heat and simmer for 2–3 minutes until the sugar is completely dissolved. Remove from the heat, leave to cool for 2 minutes, then add the basil. Leave to cool, transfer to a Mason jar and refrigerate overnight. Strain through a fine-mesh sieve and use immediately or store refrigerated in a Mason jar or other container with a tight-fitting lid.

2 Put the 2 lime wedges in the tumbler of a Boston shaker. Add the basil and sugar and muddle to release the lime juice and to crush the basil leaves. Add the syrup, ice, the juice of 1 lime wedge and rum. Shake for about 20 seconds until the shaker is beaded with sweat and very cold to the touch.

3 Pour some sugar onto a small plate. Run the remaining lime wedge around the rim of a rocks glass and dip into the sugar to coat it. Strain the rum mixture into the glass. Top with a splash of the soda water, garnish with the lime wedge used for rimming the glass and the basil sprig and serve.

Ming's tip:

The Thai basil syrup makes about 480ml, enough for 15 drinks. You can use leftover syrup to make a non-alcoholic Thai basil iced tea.

Video tip:

Watch the video to learn all about Thai basil.

Elderflower flavouring is fruity and floral. Absolut Wild Tea Vodka, used here, contains just the right amount of it and pairs naturally with cranberries – the 'Boston bog' of the drink's name. Ginger beer adds its own complementary touch to this subtly delicious drink.

ELDERFLOWER BOSTON BOG

SERVES 1

CRANBERRY-HONEY SYRUP
450g fresh cranberries
680g honey, or as needed

FOR EACH DRINK
2 heaped tablespoons cranberry–honey syrup
Juice of 1 lime
50ml Absolut Wild Tea Vodka
90ml ginger beer, preferably Gosling's
1 lime wheel

1 First make the cranberry–honey syrup. Put the cranberries in a medium saucepan. Pour in the honey until it just coats the berries. Bring to a simmer over a medium heat – 8–10 minutes – remove from the heat and leave to cool. Pour into a glass container with a snap-on lid, cover and refrigerate for up to 6 weeks.

2 Fill the tumbler of a Boston shaker with ice. Add the syrup, lime juice and vodka and shake until the shaker is beaded with sweat and very cold to the touch. Fill a highball glass with ice. Strain the vodka mixture into the glass and top with the ginger beer. Garnish with the lime wheel and serve.

Ming's tip:
You can make a delicious non-alcoholic drink by eliminating the vodka and substituting sparkling water. The cranberry–honey syrup is great on its own over ice cream – you'll have plenty left over, as this recipe yields about 700ml, enough for 30–40 drinks.

MING.COM/INYOURKITCHEN/
RECIPE79

I can't think of a better traditional cocktail than the rum- and Curaçao-based mai tai. So I set about making my own version – one with its own tropical vibe. I instantly thought of including passion fruit, which is too tart in itself, but works beautifully with other ingredients. Pineapple and orange juice plus apricot brandy further expand the fruit palette of this great drink.

PASSION FRUIT MAI TAI

SERVES 1

2 tablespoons orange juice
2 tablespoons pineapple juice
2 tablespoons passion fruit purée
1½ tablespoons gold rum, preferably Gosling's
1 tablespoon Gosling's Black Seal Rum, plus more for drizzling
1 tablespoon apricot brandy
1 tablespoon grenadine

GARNISH

1 pineapple spear (see Tips)
1 maraschino cherry
½ orange slice, notched (see Tips)

Ming's tips:

To make pineapple spears, halve a pineapple lengthways. Cut one half lengthways into 4 equal pieces, then cut each into 4 spears. Trim the spears so that they're 2.5cm longer than your highball glass. Wrap and refrigerate unused spears, which can be used for desserts or breakfast.

To prepare the orange slices, halve an orange lengthways, and cut crossways into 5mm half-moons. Notch a half-moon in the centre for fitting onto the glass rim.

1 Fill the tumbler of a Boston shaker with ice. Add the orange and pineapple juices, passion fruit purée, rums, brandy and grenadine. Shake until the shaker is beaded with sweat and very cold to the touch.

2 Fill a highball glass with ice. Strain the rum mixture into the glass and garnish with the pineapple spear, cherry and the orange half-moon. Drizzle dark rum on top and serve.

MING.COM/INYOURKITCHEN/
RECIPE80

Index

Acknowledgements

Both authors would like to thank Kyle Cathie and US publisher and editor Anja Schmidt, whose kind, attentive professionalism has made working with her a joy once again.

Ming Tsai

Thanks to my co-author Arthur Boehm who again, this fourth time, patiently and masterfully, put my passion on paper. A great writer and even better friend.

Many thanks also to chefs Joanne O'Connell and Denise Swidey, who did a spectacular job at a fierce pace for this book. Thanks also to the entire Blue Ginger crew, led by Jonathan Taylor, Tom Woods, Alex Horowitz and Matt Zikesch, and to Michele Fadden and Deanne Steffen. My gratitude as well to Blue Ginger managers Dan Adelson, Deborah Blish and Erika Staaf.

My thanks also for the super assistance provided by Jill Hardy and Lauren Klatsky—for their help with managing logistics, props and other vital matters. And gratitude to Melissa's/World Variety Produce, Inc., T.F. Kinnealey & Co., Captain Marden's Seafoods, Palm Bay International Fine Wine & Spirits, TY KU Premium Sake & Spirits, All-Clad Metalcrafters LLC, T-fal, Core Bamboo, Revol USA and Clarke showrooms for support and for providing their superior products for the shoot.

To the amazing photographer Bill 'Billy B' Bettencourt, assisted by prop stylist Aaron Caramanis, Khalilah Ramdene, Lisa Falso and Nina Gallant, many thanks for his perfect photographs. My gratitude also to videographer and media producer Steve D'Onofrio for the videos that help make this book so innovative, and Dan Kuramoto for their music.

Thanks also to my agents at IMG, Sandy Montag and Melissa Baron, for all they've done on my behalf.

Arthur Boehm

Thanks, first, to Ming Tsai, chef and friend, for the great pleasure of working with him again. In our case, more is always more.

Many thanks also to my agent, Joy Tutela of David Black Literary Agency. Gratitude also to Lauren Klatsky for her kind help in preparing the recipes for publication. And thanks again to Tama Starr for her friendship and support.